For

Red Denwick —

Please ignore some of the characters in this volume —

others you can't ignore —

and others — ?

Best wishes,

Gene Gressley

January 14, 1982

NEAR THE GREATS

AGNES WRIGHT SPRING

A PLATTE 'N PRESS BOOK

ISBN 0-939650-31-2

Denver artist Roy Hunt designed the cover for *Near the Greats.* Mr. Hunt was a friend and associate of Agnes Wright Spring while at the State Historical Society of Colorado.

PREFACE

I grew up on a ranch in Wyoming on the Little Laramie River, at the foot of Snowy Range, twenty-three miles west of Laramie.

Our ten-room log house, built by early Englishmen, was the stage stop on my father's stage and freighting lines from Laramie to Centennial and the Rambler and Keystone mines, in the Medicine Bow Range.

My older sister, Lucile, and I grew up with grownups — mine owners, miners, prospectors, stage drivers, tie hacks, cowboys, cattlemen and homesteaders.

The big folks visited with us, brought us presents and treated us as equals. I learned to like people. In later years as State Historian of Wyoming and of Colorado, I worked under nine governors, with public relations as my chief concern. True, I had my share of working with dusty bookshelves and old newspaper files, but the best of all was talking with and knowing people from a pioneer who had soldiered as a drummer at Fort Laramie in 1854 to governors and five-star generals.

Through the years I kept innumerable notes on interviews, incidents, wisps of gossip or hearsay and pertinent facts about the persons with whom I crossed trails or in whose shadows I walked. From these notes I have written what I call *Near the Greats*, with no idea of becoming a name-dropper. My only thought is to share with the reader some of the things that have interested me along the way.

Agnes Wright Spring
Fort Collins, Colorado 1981

FOREWORD

One of the gems of television's youth was the program "This Is Your Life", hosted by the "Great" Ralph Edwards. Reminiscent of that show we have, in the Foreword to *Near the Greats*, turned the tables on our author, asking some special friends, themselves "Greats", to reflect on their relationships with Agnes Wright Spring.

CAROLINE BANCROFT
Colorado Author/Historian

Agnes Wright Spring and I first met in the spring of 1945 when she joined the Western History Department of the Denver Public Library. From that day to this we have maintained a warm personal and professional friendship, sharing historical knowledge and confidential opinions about co-workers.

Her career has been marked by many achievements and awards, perhaps the most notable being that she is the only person in the United States to have been the official state historian of two states — Wyoming and Colorado. While holding the latter position, she edited the historical society's *Colorado Magazine* and wrote some of the book reviews. It was then that she published a criticism of my first version of ***Denver's Lively Past***. In it, I had stated that "5280 feet" was painted on the exact step of that height on the west side steps of the state capitol building. Instead of noting this in her criticism, she phoned me and told me to go look at the step. The legend was *carved* into the riser, not painted. Agnes had saved me any public humiliation by her always consistent kindness. (Of course, the error was corrected in the next edition.)

DR. GENE M. GRESSLEY
Assistant to the President, University of Wyoming

To remember Agnes Wright Spring is to recall the first time that I saw her. It was on a beautiful, sunny afternoon in the Colorado autumn of 1952. As a twenty-one year old historian, fresh from commencement, I needed a job — desperately. My wife, Joyce, was in graduate school at the University of Colorado. Newly married, I was seeking employment, after the surprising development of flunking my army physical. I walked up to Mrs. Spring's apartment door on Sherman Street in Denver, and timidly knocked. When the door opened, the lady who greeted me was to be my "boss" for the next two years, and to have a major influence on my life and career.

For I discovered Agnes Wright Spring, as have all others, an amazingly knowledgeable historian, an intensely warm person, and above all else a totally selfless individual. Legends abound about the help she has freely given to one and all over the years. The torn piece of paper that arrives in the mail, containing a reference to an article in the *Rocky Mountain News* for 1882. The putting in of a good word at the crucial spot and time. Again, as so often with others, I benefitted from her unreserved and enthusiastic recommendation. Desiring to return to the Rockies in the spring of 1956, I wrote Mrs. Spring. Soon she was on the phone to friends in Wyoming, and shortly thereafter my family and I were bound for a job at the University of Wyoming.

The fact that this neophyte historian and the Wyoming opportunity developed as well as they did was again due in large measure to the background that the former Ladies Golf Champion of Wyoming furnished me. During brown bag lunch hours at the Colorado State Historical Society (frequently interrupted by a donor wanting to present that "smiling" lady with an arrowhead, or a miner's candleholder) Mrs. Spring regaled me with the legends and lore that are Wyoming. How often I recalled, with profit, those stories, vignettes and anecdotes over the coming years, as I criss-crossed "our" state. How often that background saved me from an embarrassing faux pas or revealed ignorance.

Yes, I shall always remember Agnes Wright Spring with more affection and gratitude than I can ever express. She will remain Mrs. Spring to me, for as a youngster in knickers, I was taught to address my superiors formally — by last name. Mrs. Spring will ever be my superior, and ever be remembered as a marvelously dedicated and warmly generous human being.

LUCILLE HASTINGS
President, Denver Woman's Press Club

Agnes Wright Spring has perpetuated Colorado history of events and people in her carefully detailed writing as few others have done so well. We who know her and read her writings learn a greater appreciation of our Colorado heritage. Even more than that, during the years she was historian of two states, Wyoming and Colorado, a unique attainment in America, she has given unselfishly of her time, effort and talents to help others in research and writing. Her countless admiring appreciative readers pay tribute to her historical literary contributions, also to her modesty and kindness to all her many friends and acquaintances. She is one of Colorado's GREATS.

DEAN KRAKEL
Executive Vice President, National Cowboy Hall of Fame

I admire Agnes Wright Spring as much as anyone I know. She has influenced my professional life enormously.

When I was a flunkie at Colorado Historical Society and Mrs. Spring was the State Historian, we joked around a great deal and came up with a corny little limerick about our boss, because she was invariably out of her office interviewing some old-timer or collecting some artifact for the museum:

Spring is sprung,
The grass is riz,
There's work to be done,
We wonder where Agnes is?

DR. NOLIE MUMEY
Colorado Author/Historian

Agnes Wright Spring, a very talented lady with a retentive memory for historical events, is one of the greatest of Colorado women. Her knowledge of this state and of Wyoming is astounding. Mrs. Spring is an accurate researcher and an interesting writer of Western Americana, having many publications to her credit.

PAT WAGNER
Editor, *Western Publications*

Remember the lettuceworm gauge of politeness? If the little beast is on your salad plate, hide it under a leaf if you can; if not, eat it quickly before the hostess notices. I think Agnes Wright Spring would consider going that far to spare somebody's feelings.

She and her husband were in our town one year when the weather was a sweltering 90 degrees. Mr. Spring unexpectedly came down with chills. The hotel could block off their room's air conditioning and offer blankets, but that was all, so we dug out a space heater from our office basement.

What we weren't prepared for, when we delivered it, was seeing Agnes waiting out in front, dressed in a heavy wool suit.

She might smile in denial, but I have always believed that when she carried that heater into the room, the conversation might have gone something like this:

"Archer, isn't this great? I didn't want to mention it till you did, but I've been absolutely freezing too. Now we can *both* be comfortable!"

That's love.

NELLIE SNYDER YOST
Western Author/Historian

I have long admired writer-historian Agnes Wright Spring, a delightful, friendly lady. My most vivid recollection of her deals with an incident that occurred at the 1977 Western Writers of America convention in Oklahoma City, to which she was accompanied by her brother-in-law, Howard Fish. On the opening evening some 100 members were transported by bus to the Liberty National Bank for a banquet in the Petroleum Club's dining room on the top floor. After an elegant repast the members divided into two groups, one to return to the hotel, and bed, the other to visit the moonlit gardens of the Cowboy Hall of Fame.

When the buses were finally loaded it was discovered that Mr. Fish was missing. Agnes and her fellow members, fearing that he might have had a heart attack in an elevator, rest room or stairway, wouldn't leave without him. An ambulance was called to stand by while younger members of the writers group, assisted by the Pinkerton operatives in charge of security for the vast building, combed its thirty-six floors. Finally the city police were called in and the search intensified.

Meanwhile the jolly Mr. Fish, having struck up a friendship with a carload of non WWA members who were also visiting the Cowboy Hall of Fame, had accepted their invitation to ride along. While the frantic search was in progress back at the bank, he was happily strolling the magnificent gardens, where a policeman, who finally thought to check there, found him. Agnes, after all her fright and worry, forgave him, laughed about the whole ridiculous incident, and bought and presented a $25.00 bottle of fine wine to the helpful Pinkerton men who had so ably assisted in the great Fish hunt.

There is little we can add to these commendations of Agnes Wright Spring, except to say it has been a privilege for us to work Near a Great.

John and Eleanor Ayer
JENDE-HAGAN BOOKCORP

TABLE OF CONTENTS

Franklin P. Adams 1
Ramon F. Adams 3
Susan B. Anthony 4
Thurman Arnold 6
Fay Bainter 7
Jim Baker 8
Captain Harvey Barnum 9
Amelia Barr 10
William E. Barrett 11
Queen Anne Bassett (Willis) 11
Lew Bates 12
Lucius Beebe 13
Charles Belden 14
Mary Godat Bellamy 15
Roy Best 17
Black Kettle's Widow 18
Nathaniel K. Boswell 19
Walter Brennan 20
Mrs. J.J. Brown "Unsinkable Molly Brown" 22
Struthers Burt 23
Nicholas Murray Butler 24
Goldie Cameron 24
Jane Canary - Calamity Jane 25
Joseph "Josie" M. Carey & Louisa M.D. Carey 26
John B. Kendrick 30
Frank L. Houx 31
Bill Carlisle 33
Kit Carson III 33
Butch Cassidy 34
Carrie Chapman Catt 35
William F. Cody - Buffalo Bill 37
Dane Coolidge 40
Grace Coolidge 40
Jane Cowl 41
Homer Croy 41

General George Custer 43
William C. Deming 44
Thomas A. Dewey 47
Dr. June E. Downey 47
Wesley Dumm 48
Marcel Dumont 49
Mrs. Boney Earnest - "Aunt Mat" 52
Ralph Edwards 53
Mamie Eisenhower 55
John Evans 57
Luther K. Evans 59
Douglas Fairbanks 60
Maude Fealy 61
Vardis Fisher 62
Bennett Foster 63
Will Geer 63
Vance Graham 65
Ulysses Sumner Grant 66
Dr. Gene M. Gressley 66
Charles Guernsey 67
Dr. LeRoy Hafen 68
Walter Hagen 69
Gordon Langley Hall 70
Averill Harriman 70
John Hawgood 71
William Randolph Hearst 71
Dr. Grace Raymond Hebard 72
Chris Holley 77
Herbert Hoover 78
Tom Horn 79
John-O Hoskins 83
Andy Huff 84
Frazier Hunt 85
John Hunton 87
William H. Jackson 88
Jesse James III 89
Governor Edwin Johnson 90
Mrs. Frank "Rainwater" Jones 90
General Charles King 92
Dr. Samuel Howell Knight 92
Dean Krakel 94

Homer Lea 95
E. Hamilton Lee 96
Colonel Charles Lindbergh 97
J.C. Lobato 98
Earnest A. Logan 98
Robert Lorenz 100
Robert S. McAuley 103
Tim McCoy 105
Mrs. Gus Craven - Denver McGaa's Daughter 108
Governor Steve McNichols 110
Andrew Manseau 110
Elwood Mead 111
"Doc" Middleton 112
General Bernard Montgomery 113
Mrs. Annie D. Morris 114
Mrs. Esther Morris 115
Dr. Nolie Mumey 115
James Murray 116
John Myers Myers 117
Wiley Oakley 119
Donald R. Ornduff 120
Governor John Osborne 122
G. Edward Pendray 123
General John J. Pershing 123
Walter B. Pitkin 125
Garrett Price 126
Professor Michael Idvorsky Pupin 126
William McLeod Raine 127
Jeannette Rankin 127
Alice Hegan Rice 128
Rev. John Roberts 128
Dr. James Grafton Rogers 132
"Sissy" Root 136
Nellie Tayloe Ross 137
Mari Sandoz 138
Jack Schaefer 138
M. Lincoln Schuster 139
Willard Simms 140
Colonel George Sliney 141
Dr. E.E. Slosson 141
May Bonfils Berryman Stanton 142

Irving Stone 145
Michael Straight 145
Henry Swan 146
R.W. Thaler 148
Lowell Thomas 149
Dan Thornton 151
Russell Thorp 152
Pancho Villa 154
Baron Von Richthofen's Family 155
Martha Bull Waln 156
Dr. Agnes M. Wergeland 158
Meredith Wilson and Reni 160
Duchess of Windsor 160
William Wright - Dan De Quille 161
Pete Wollery 161

NEAR THE GREATS

AGNES WRIGHT SPRING

FRANKLIN P. ADAMS

N THE AUTUMN of 1916, I had a desk in the "City Room" of the Pulitzer School of Journalism, Columbia University, in New York City.

Having never been east of Denver, I listened intently, almost with awe to the conversations of my classmates as they discussed the events of the day, criticized the grand opera prima donna, or discussed our assignments. Daily they quoted or mentioned what F.P.A. had said.

"Who is F.P.A.?" I ventured.

"He's the best columnist of today," the young man at the next desk told me. "His name is Franklin P. Adams."

From then on I read and enjoyed F.P.A.'s column. It was not until some months later that I ran across a letter of introduction that Margaret Bailey of Cheyenne, Wyoming had given to me. I battled many a golf game with her but did not know her friends. I stared at the envelope she had given me. It was addressed to "Mrs. Franklin P. Adams -- Dear Minna --."

How, I wondered, did Margaret know the wife of such an eminent New York newspaperman?

I hesitated to present the letter at that date. It was long after I left Columbia and returned to Wyoming that I learned why Margaret and many other Wyoming folk knew Minna Adams.

In doing research on the old Cheyenne and Black Hills Trail, I discovered that Minna was the daughter of Fred M. Schwartze, who owned a stage stop and cattle ranch on Pole Creek, eighteen miles north of Cheyenne. Schwartze began ranching there in 1871, and owned several hundred head of cattle and horses.

As a young woman, Minna had gone on the legitimate stage and while playing in the "Flora Dora Girl," in Chicago, had met a young news reporter, F.P. Adams. They were married and went to New York to live.

Friends recalled that Minna used to tell about a cowboy fracas at the Pole Creek ranch, when she was very small. The memory of the affair had remained vivid with her through the years. She said, "A storm was brewing that late autumn day and every man on the ranch, including the bartender, had been pressed into service to help with the haying. Mrs. Isaac Bard, from a neighboring ranch, arrived with some friends for a little visit with Mrs. Schwartze. While the latter was preparing some coffee in the big dining room, there suddenly was some shooting in the barroom adjoining. The guests and two Swedish 'hired girls' ran down the long porch from the kitchen headed for the willows along the 'crick'. Mrs. Schwartze being large with child moved more slowly. She lifted Minna, then about three years old, to her shoulder and started to follow the others. Then came a shot through the dining room door, which hit the china door knob. The bullet was deflected across the room.

"A six-foot Texan," says Minna, "with a cocked gun came into the room, very drunk and me looking straight into his gun! Mama whirled around and said to him, 'What do you want?' 'We want your liquor,' he said. 'Go out to the barroom and get it,' my mother told him. All the time shooting was going on in the barroom. The man was very drunk and lurched towards my mother. She took him by the collar and marched him through the door. I can still see the face leering at me, with a gun a few inches from my face."

Mrs. Schwartze, with Minna, joined the others in the willows where they remained until the stage came in.

That night Mrs. Schwartze was taken very ill. Her child was born dead. Efforts to track down and arrest the miscreants were fruitless.

The story called "Rollicking Rioters" appeared in the *Police Gazette* in New York City in 1882.

In later years F.P.A. and Minna separated. He was a well-known radio broadcaster on "Information Please." He died on March 23, 1960; Minna lived out her years a semi-invalid in Washington, D.C. She kept in touch with old Wyoming friends who shared her letters with me.

I always regretted that I did not present my letter of introduction to "Dear Minna."

RAMON F. ADAMS

LONG RECOGNIZED as the foremost bibliographer and lexicographer of the West, Ramon F. Adams of Dallas, Texas, was one of the most appreciative, co-operative persons with whom I worked in the western history field. A tall, dark Texan he was soft-spoken, friendly and had a keen sense of humor. He was more zealous in running down an elusive western word or expression than any cowboy who cut mavericks out of the brush in the Panhandle.

For years we carried on a lively correspondence. Later, my husband and I came to know Ramon personally when he spent a week or more in Denver checking the books in the State Historical Society of Colorado and the Western History Department of the Denver Public Library.

I came to know Ramon and Allie Adams best, however, when I was a guest in their Dallas home.

While I was at the Crazy Water Hotel in Mineral Wells, Texas taking treatments for arthritis, I received an invitation to come to Dallas to visit the owners of the Allie Adams Candy Company.

I avoid visiting in private homes, if possible; I suppose it is just a phobia, as I do not want to discommode my hosts. But I did not hesitate to accept this invitation from Ramon and Allie.

My welcome was most cordial. The walls of the Adams' home were quite interesting with the beautiful plates which Allie had collected. Ramon explained that whenever he bought an expensive book, he bought Allie a plate, particularly when he was traveling.

Ramon had a most impressive collection of western books — rare and valuable, which I certainly enjoyed inspecting.

At bedtime Allie explained that she was going to move into Ramon's room with him and would give me her room for the night. She said that her pet cat had never spent the night anywhere else, so would share the room with me. "I hope you won't mind having him," she finished.

Mr. Cat was a beautiful Siamese, the biggest one of its kind I had ever seen. He planted himself erect at the side of my bed. He did not take his eyes off me.

I retired as soon as possible and ducked under the covers. Now and then I would come up for air, but Mr. Cat was plainly in view in the moonlight. I was greatly relieved when it came time for me to join Ramon and Allie for breakfast. I assured Allie she had a *beautiful* cat! I had never seen one like him.

Ramon was perhaps the most dedicated researcher I ever knew. His goal was accuracy and completeness.

When the University of Oklahoma published his first book on "Western Words," he sent me a copy with his autograph which read: "To Agnes Wright Spring. I ride in your dust." His language was always colorful and meaningful -- and Western.

In the Appreciation in his first edition he wrote: "The authors I quote are not the town-gaited writers who have never been closer to a cow than a milk wagon. They have lived the life, and you may have confidence in their knowledge. I extend thanks to the following writers each of whom I am proud to list as a personal friend: J. Frank Dobie, W.S. Campbell (Stanley Vestal), Edward Everett Dale, J. Evetts Haley, Foster-Harris, William McLeod Raine, Agnes Wright Spring, Jack Porter, John M. Hendrix and the late George Saunders."

Ramon Adams wrote books and articles, many of them. One of my favorites was "Come an' Get It."

Ramon passed away in the spring of 1977. The last time I saw him was at a convention of the Western History Association in Tucson, Arizona in October, 1968. I was having dinner in a small nook at the hotel when several of my good historian friends arrived for the convention. All of them greeted me with shouts of surprise and welcome. Ramon stepped forward, leaned over and kissed me -- a sincere tribute from a real *Great!*

SUSAN B. ANTHONY

SUSAN B. ANTHONY'S photograph, in her later years, looked enough like my paternal grandmother, Mrs. Isaac Wright, to be a sister. But Susan was not a blood kin. Perhaps it was their hairstyle. Susan's uncle married an aunt of my father, Gordon L. Wright, so she was only "in the family." Aunt Molly, Dad's sister, used to tell me about Susan, whom she met when she visited in Iowa.

Susan was not the severe, mannish type so often portrayed as a woman's rights advocate. Susan wore a sealskin coat and blue ribbons on her bonnet. She enjoyed good food, and was especially fond of steak. I knew, and often talked with a friend of Miss

Anthony, Theresa Jenkins of Cheyenne, Wyoming, who was an ardent supporter of equal rights and worked hard to obtain statehood for Wyoming.

Mrs. Jenkins told me how that long ago, before loudspeakers were in use, she developed a strong speaking voice. She was in demand as a speaker in many places because she could be heard.

Mrs. Jenkins said that she and her husband Horace used to go in their buggy out to the prairie near Cheyenne. He would sit in the buggy and listen while she walked farther and farther away from him, while making a speech. In that way she developed her voice.

Horace Jenkins was a Deputy U.S. Marshal, and escorted Jack McCall, the killer of Wild Bill Hickok, from Cheyenne to prison in Yankton, Dakota Territory.

In early Colorado and Wyoming newspapers I found many references to Susan B.'s speaking tours to the remote mining towns and elsewhere. Susan had grit and stamina.

In 1965, Dr. Ray A. Billington, nationally known historian and research associate of the Huntington Library, San Marino, California, recommended me for an $800.00 research grant for two months to study the papers of Susan B. Anthony in the Huntington Library.

I had crossed trails many times with Ray Billington as a member of historical groups, in research work, in studying his writings, and in meeting Mabel and Ray Billington at historical conventions.

Dr. Ray Billington has, I'm sure, more degrees and scholastic honors from universities and colleges than any of my "Greats." He holds degrees from eleven institutions of higher learning, including the Universities of Wisconsin, Michigan, Harvard and Oxford. He is an authority on Frederick Jackson Turner and many other subjects.

The opportunity to study at Huntington Library, which Dr. Ray made possible to me, was wonderful. I examined all of the papers of Susan B. Anthony which the Huntington Library holds and intend someday to complete my work on Miss Anthony.

The recently minted Susan B. Anthony dollar pays tribute to a really Great woman.

THURMAN ARNOLD

WHEN I WAS about nine years old my older sister, Lucile, and I attended school in Laramie, Wyoming and lived at 715 Grand Avenue with our Grandmother Wright, and two aunts, Mary and Agnes Wright, teachers in the Laramie schools. Our close neighbors were the Arnolds, Corthells, Knights and Slossons. There were about a dozen youngsters in "our gang."

In September, 1903, an early snow storm struck Laramie, before the leaves had fallen. The weight of the wet snow broke hundreds of limbs from trees. When George Morgan, the local drayman, began to load his wagon to carry the leaves away, we swarmed him and begged him to dump the limbs on the large vacant lot back of the Corthell house. We planned to build an Indian village.

During the summer Mrs. Nellis Corthell had taken her eight children, Thurman, Morris, Evelyn, Miriam, Gladys, Robin, Huron and Irving in a covered wagon from Laramie to the Yellowstone Park. On their return trip they had visited the Wind River Indian Reservation near Lander. There they had witnessed a Sun Dance being performed in a Sun Dance Lodge. Mrs. Corthell bought a small Indian pony, which her boys named Washakie and on which they took turns riding.

Robin, who had a tree house in the Corthell back yard, directed our lodge-building work. Like a swarm of bees we carried the tree limbs to the center of the lot while the older boys put up the lodge. Twelve-year-old Thurman Arnold, self-appointed Chief, took command and our Sun Dance began. The boys pranced back and forth from the center pole, while the girls shuffled in a circle, chanting weird noises. Thurman took great glee in seizing one of my long pigtails and tying me up to the Sun Dance pole for scalping.

Laramie being a small town of only about 3,000 persons everyone soon learned of our Indian performances and village.

We were asked to perform at the Albany County Fair just beginning about a mile from the town limits. Eagerly we trailed on foot to the race track in front of the "grandstand." With home-made tom toms we went into our dance. The local newspapers called us the "Corthell Indians." I remember well my long blue flowered wrapper and moccasins.

How could we know that Chief Thurman Arnold would continue his scalping proclivities and become a nationally known "trust buster" with Abe Fortas in Washington, D.C.? Or, that Huron would participate in the construction of the Golden Gate Bridge over San Francisco Bay? Or, that Robin would make a name for himself as a designer and builder of ships on the Pacific Coast? Sam Knight became internationally known as a geologist and little Carl Arnold was a one-time Dean of the Law School at the University of Wyoming. They were all *Greats*!

FAY BAINTER

N THE SUMMER of 1916, I was enrolled as a junior in the Pulitzer School of Journalism, Columbia University, New York City.

One of my thrills in the City was to play golf on the beautiful golf course at Van Cortlandt Park. I had learned the game on rough polo grounds adjoining Fort D.A. Russell at Cheyenne, Wyoming. We thought nothing of digging our balls out of prairie dog holes. Our greens were sand and most of our fairways were ROUGH.

On weekdays at Van Cortlandt Park there was a so-called "bag line", which determined the matching of partners. One morning the bag next to mine was owned by a fine looking, athletic young man who said he had no objection to playing with a woman. We teed off.

In Wyoming comparatively few women played golf, and I had learned to play with men and one woman, who helped me with my game.

When I told my new partner that I was from Wyoming he said that he had been a brakeman on the Union Pacific Railroad between Rawlins and Green River in Wyoming. His name was Nelson.

After we had played a few holes he said he was now an actor on Broadway, the Captain in "East is West," in which Fay Bainter was starring.

I told him I would like to interview her for my work in journalism.

"Fine," he said. "Here is my card. All you have to do is go to the stage door and ask to see Miss Bainter."

The following Saturday afternoon, I presented the Captain's

card and was admitted to Miss Bainter's dressing room.

Miss Bainter was very cordial and talked freely. She said she had been walking home from the theater to save taxi fare and had been donating what she saved to charities.

A great story! I hurried to our "City Room" at the School of Journalism to write my interview. With much satisfaction I turned the story in to my professor.

Imagine my chagrin when the manuscript came back marked "D - Why don't you get something original?"

Then I discovered that this story had been in all of the newspapers. Miss Bainter had a stereotyped "interview" ready for all comers! I had a D -- but to me it should have been an "A".

The only time I saw the "Captain" again was in "East is West."

JIM BAKER

When I answered my State Historian's telephone one morning, a voice asked, "Are Jim Baker's children buried in my back yard?" I asked for his address and when he told me, said, "No. They are buried on a ditch bank about four doors down the street from you."

"I'm glad," said the man. "I wanted to build a shed and I didn't want to disturb 'em."

Now Jim Baker, early day scout, ferry owner and pioneer, had left his cabin and store on Clear Creek on the edge of Denver more than eighty or eighty-five years before. He built a block house on the Little Snake River near Savery, Wyoming. The block house now stands at the gate of Frontier Park in Cheyenne, Wyoming.

The question of the graves of the three Baker children had been called to the attention of the State Historical Society by someone proposing to have the Society mark the graves and make an entrance to them for visitors.

Dr. and Mrs. James Grafton Rogers and I had found the graves on a ditch bank owned by the Rio Grande Gravel Company about 100 yards back of a residence on west 58th Avenue. A few little stones and some cactus were above the graves. The spot had almost been covered by blowing earth.

A check of records in the city clerk's office produced proof that when Jim Baker sold his cabin and land along Clear Creek, he stipulated that the three graves should never be disturbed. His shadow still seemed to hover over the place. I had visited his own grave, marked by a shaft on a rolling hillside near Savery, Wyoming. In his day Jim Baker had taken part in the Indian fight at Battle Mountain and had scouted the West. He was almost as well-known to pioneers as Jim Bridger.

Dr. Rogers advised that we should not approve the erection of a monument over the graves that might attract visitors, since the only access would be across private property. I trust that Jim Baker's wish is still being carried out.

CAPTAIN HARVEY BARNUM

IT WAS FLAG DAY, June 14, 1966. The Leyden-Chiles Post of the American Legion in Denver was putting on a celebration in the park in front of the State Capitol. According to the program the speaker of the day was to be Captain Harvey Barnum of the Marines, a Congressional Medal of Honor man. I had been invited to sit on the platform to receive an award for my work as State Historian.

James Eakin, post commander, escorted me to the platform where the Captain in a white suit wore a blue ribbon suspending the Medal of Honor around his neck. He greeted me with a smile. After we had taken our seats side by side, he whispered, "Watch--a General has to salute the wearer of a Congressional Medal--army regulations."

Then he stood up and his fun began. Four or five Generals came up the steps to the platform and ceremoniously saluted the Captain. They were from the U.S. Air Force Academy, from Lowry Field, and from Fitzsimmons.

I believe I was nearly as thrilled as the Captain. Harvey Barnum had rescued fourteen of his marine comrades under fire.

He gave an inspirational talk aimed at the youth in the audience.

After a plaque was presented to me and I took my seat, Captain Harvey Barnum placed one arm over my shoulder and said, "You deserve it."

Whoever thought being an historian was dull business?

The citation given Captain Harvey Barnum, Jr., according to *Medal of Honor Recipients* 1863-1973 follows:

HARVEY C. BARNUM, Jr. Rank and Regulation: Captain, United States Marine Corps, Company H, Second Battalion 9th

Marines, 3rd. Marine Division Reinforced. Place and date: Ky Phu in Quang Tin Province, Republic of Vietnam, 18 December, 1965. Entered service at Cheshire, Conn. Date and place of birth: July 21, 1940. Waterbury, Conn. Citation: For conspicuous gallantry and intrepidity at the risk of his life above and beyond the call of duty. When the company was suddenly pinned down by an extremely accurate enemy fire and was quickly separated from the remainder of the battalion by over five hundred metres of open and fire-swept ground and casualties mounted rapidly, Lieutenant Barnum quickly made a hazardous reconnaissance of the area, seeking targets for the artillery. Finding the rifle company commander mortally wounded and the radio operator killed, he, with complete disregard for his own safety, gave aid to the dying commander, then removed the radio from the dead operator, and strapped it to himself. He immediately assumed command of the rifle company, and moved at once into the midst of the heavy fire, rallying and giving encouragement to all units, reorganizing them to replace the loss of key personnel and led the attack on enemy positions from which deadly fire continued to come. His sound and swift decisions and his obvious calm served to stabilize the badly decimated units and his gallant example as he stood exposed repeatedly to point out targets served as an inspiration to all. Provided with two armed helicopters, he moved fearlessly through to control the air attack against the firmly entrenched enemy while skillfully directing one platoon in a successful counter attack on the key enemy positions. Having thus cleared a small area, he requested and directed the landing of two transport helicopters for the evacuation of the dead and wounded. He then assisted in the mopping up and final seizure of the battalion's objective. His gallant initiative and heroic conduct reflected great credit upon himself and were in keeping with the highest traditions of the Marine Corps and United States Naval Service.

I am proud to have Captain Barnum's photograph on my living room table.

AMELIA BARR

AS A STUDENT at the School of Journalism, Columbia University, I eagerly accepted an assignment to interview Amelia Barr, well-known novelist, who at 82 years was still writing books, especially for girls. She received me at her home out on Long Island, where I spent a delightful afternoon. She was cordial and very alert and seemed to enjoy telling me about her writing work through the years. One of the things she impressed on me was that a writer should write -- not dream about writing. She was a real inspiration to an embryonic journalist.

WILLIAM E. BARRETT

ONE OF MY favorite authors, as a writer and as a person, is William E. Barrett of Denver, whom I have known as a fellow member of the Colorado Authors' League for many years. I thrilled over his "Left Hand of God," and again over "The Lilies of the Field."

Most of all have I been pleased to own a copy of "The Lotus Lady," his latest book. It must have been thirty years ago that I sat next to William E. Barrett at a banquet. We were talking about writing when he said that there was a story he hoped to write some day called "The Lotus Lady;" a story about Buddha's wife. During the years that followed, Bill Barrett visited foreign lands, studied religious records, talked with priests and laymen in gathering data for his book. It is a real masterpiece which alone places him among the Greats.

QUEEN ANNE BASSETT (WILLIS)

QUEEN ANNE BASSETT of Brown's Hole, was a favorite subject of western writers for some time, and still is. She was the daughter of a pioneer settler in Brown's Hole in the far northwestern corner of Colorado, which was frequented by outlaws and those who were "on the run." Queen Anne was educated in a woman's college in the east, but returned to ranch life. When she was accused of cattle rustling, she developed a fierce hatred for the big cattle outfits. She insisted that she was innocent of rustling. A court dismissed the charge.

In trying to figure out how she could get even with the big cattlemen, she decided that she would marry Hi Bernard, the foreman of one of the biggest outfits. She did. Their married life was stormy and eventually they separated.

When I was State Historian of Colorado, I received a letter from Arthur Corcoran, a western writer, who was then living in Canon

City, Colorado. Corcoran said that he would like to have me get the record straight for our files. He claimed that Queen Anne of Brown's Hole had agreed to let him write her biography. He stated that he spent a great deal of time writing the story. During the work on the story, Queen Anne took him to the grave of Hi Bernard. According to Corcoran she stomped on the grave and called Hi many unprintable names.

Later she took the manuscript away from Corcoran and insisted that she had written it herself. A story "written by Anne Bassett Willis" was published in *The Colorado Magazine*, official publication of the Historical Society of Colorado, Vol. 29 and Vol. 30. All Arthur Corcoran asked of me was to make his side of the story known. So here it is.

LEW BATES

IN THE LATE 1930's a young reporter for the *Wyoming Eagle* in Cheyenne, Wyoming, named Lew Bates, used to drop by regularly at the Federal Writers' Project. I liked him. I like the way he wrote. He was one of the local reporters who seemed to be interested in coming to our office. Some of the reporters considered us just a "boon-doggling outfit."

One morning when I reached my office after a weekend in Fort Collins, Colorado, Lew Bates was there. Suddenly an idea struck me.

"I have a scoop for you," I said. "Last night in Fort Collins, Ruth Warren told me that Johnny Wellborn, a young Denver financier, had given a diamond ring to Mary Helen Warren, Ruth's cousin. We had all attended a party the week before at Ruth's home."

"Mary Helen Warren," I told Lew Bates, "is the granddaughter of U.S. Senator Francis E. Warren, the daughter of Fred Warren, president of the Warren Livestock Company, and the Wyoming Stock Growers, and she is a niece of 'Black Jack' Pershing. She was home on vacation when we were at Ruth's party."

As I finished talking Lew Bates was off to the races. He went straight to the Fred Warren home in Cheyenne. Mrs. Warren came to the door.

Lew asked to speak with Mary Helen.

"What do you want?" Mrs. Warren asked. "Mary Helen is in Palo Alto. What did you want to ask her?"

"About her engagement to Johnny Wellborn."

"Nonsense. My daughter is not engaged." Mrs. Warren was positive.

But when Lew insisted that Johnny had given her a diamond ring, Mrs. Warren immediately telephoned to California.

Mary Helen confirmed the engagement.

Very shortly Lew's story was on the *Wyoming Eagle's* press. He scooped the Denver newspapers. Johnny and Mary Helen Warren were married in due time and bought a ranch in Wyoming near Pinedale.

Lew Bates no longer was a cub. He steadily advanced until in about 1940 he was managing editor of the *Wyoming Tribune.*

Our Federal Writers' Project completed and published the "Wyoming Guide," thanks to the help of two excellent writers, Dee Linford and Richard Rossiter and other staff members.

Some years went by during which we received praise for the work on the "Guide." An ambitious legislator, however, began to promote the idea of appropriating some $50,000 to have a guidebook of Wyoming written.

Lew Bates wrote a magnificent editorial article in which he asked why a new guidebook was needed. He said our "Wyoming Guide" was quite sufficient. No appropriation was made.

That editorial by Lew Bates was the finest tribute that could be paid to those of us who had worked so hard to produce the Guide.

LUCIUS BEEBE

LUCIUS BEEBE, New York City socialite and society reporter, came often with his friend, Charles M. Clegg, to do research in the Western History Department of the Denver Public Library when I was assisting there under Ina Aulls, head. Alys Freeze was Miss Aulls' assistant.

Lucius was gathering data to write a history of narrow gauge railways in Colorado. The Western History Department which had been established by Dr. Malcolm Wyer, librarian of the Denver Public Library, was rich in railway materials, including photographs.

Beebe was a tall, good-looking man who affected western garb with a cutaway coat, large flashy tie, and a gold log chain for his watch dangling across his middle.

Miss Aulls and Alys helped with the research. I was an onlooker.

At Christmastime our staff enjoyed the large box of Delicious apples which Lucius sent to Miss Aulls from his orchard in Washington. I think it was in the Wenatchee Valley.

All western railway "buffs" are familiar with the books which Lucius Beebe wrote. They are now collector's items.

When Beebe went to Virginia City, Nevada, and purchased and published the *Territorial Enterprise*, the old newspaper originally run by Mark Twain and William Wright (Dan De Quille), I wrote him and told him that Dan De Quille was my father's cousin. I asked him if he would be interested in an unpublished manuscript of Dan's which had been in our family for ages. He wrote that he would be and I sent it to him.

Lucius owned a private railway car in which he and Clegg took trips all over the country.

In 1970, Alys Freeze and I attended a convention of the Western History Association held in Reno, Nevada. She was then head of the Western History Department, as Miss Aulls had retired. Alys asked me to join her party of five to visit Clegg in the Victorian house in Virginia City, which he had inherited from Lucius Beebe.

We drove from Reno to Virginia City late one afternoon and were graciously received by Charles Clegg. He served champagne and hors d'ouvres, then gave us free rein to inspect the house.

The library of books was magnificent! Priceless! The details of the house furnishings were remarkable. No expense had been spared to make the restoration accurate and beautiful.

Our host told us that he was having the special car serviced down in Sparks, Nevada preparatory to a trip to San Francisco. I think he said it would cost $300.00 just to attach the car to the train. It might have been $3,000.00! I'm not sure.

At any rate it was a rare privilege to visit the Victorian house once owned by Lucius Beebe, who had died on February 4, 1966.

CHARLES BELDEN

HARLES BELDEN of the Pitchfork Ranch, near Meeteetse, Wyoming, husband of Frances Phelps Belden, was in his day the outstanding photographer of cowboys, cattle, horses, ranch life, and wildlife in Wyoming. In fact, he caught all phases of the Old West in his lenses. He had a studio at his ranch.

My husband and I went to the Pitchfork hoping to see Charles Belden to obtain illustrations for the "Wyoming Guide."

We were disappointed to find him away, but Mrs. Belden was most gracious and invited us to have dinner with her. It was the day following Thanksgiving and we had a real feast with turkey and all of the trimmings. Mrs. Belden was the daughter of Louis Graham Phelps, owner of the Phelps Land and Cattle Company, whose holdings eventually reached 250,000 acres. In 1903 Phelps bought the Pitchfork Ranch from the estate of Otto Franc.

The Belden home was richly furnished with Oriental rugs, paintings, china and crystal. Through the large picture window we could see deer grazing in the meadow.

We told Mrs. Belden what photographs we desired and later Charles sent some splendid ones to us.

I understood that later the Beldens separated and Charles went to Florida to live. One day he came into my office in the State Museum in Denver. He asked if I would write an article about a sheep wagon that could be illustrated with some photographs which he had. He said he thought he could sell it to *Collier's* or some national magazine.

I really worked hard on the article and sent it to Belden. A year or so went by with no word from him. Then I discovered the well-illustrated article in the *Western Livestock Magazine*, published in Denver. It won a Top Hand award in its class in the annual contest of the Colorado Authors' League. The photographs won the award, I'm sure.

In 1978, Frances Phelps Belden, then 89 years old, still living at the Pitchfork Ranch, was featured in a magnificently illustrated book called "Brand of a Legend", by Bob Edgar and Jack Turnell. It is a thrilling book to own.

MARY GODAT BELLAMY

MARY GODAT BELLAMY, of Laramie, Wyoming, wife of Charles Bellamy, was the first woman to be elected to the State Legislative Assembly of Wyoming in 1910 and served in the 1911 session.

Mrs. Bellamy had a brilliant mind and was a leader in many civic and state affairs. Her husband, Charles, a Bostonian, a skilled engineer, held the No. 1 license issued to engineers in Wyoming.

Probably few persons know about Mary G. winning a story contest a long time ago which netted a $500.00 prize. A magazine which ran an unfinished story offered the prize to the persons who sent in the best conclusion to the story. With the $500.00, Mrs. Bellamy invested in Union Pacific Railway stock. She told me that she kept the stock through the years and that it increased a great deal in value.

Mrs. Bellamy was very proud of the fact that when she was in the legislature she was instrumental in saving the Agricultural College for the University of Wyoming -- keeping all colleges in Laramie. Lander fought very hard to get the Agricultural College. Mrs. Bellamy dictated to me the story of how she won the political fight.

She knew Esther Morris, who had been appointed the justice of the peace at South Pass City, whose statue is in front of Wyoming's Capitol and Statuary Hall in Washington, D.C. Mrs. Bellamy told me that when Esther Morris lived in Laramie with her son, Edward Slack, she used to take a baby buggy and go down to the Union Pacific tracks and pick up pieces of coal and take them to poor families.

Mrs. Bellamy's sons, Benjamin and Fulton, were among Wyoming's most substantial citizens.

Her grandson, John C., son of Benjamin, now a professor at the University of Wyoming, became a weather expert and broadcast the weather for Jimmy Doolittle when he dropped the bomb over Hiroshima in April, 1942.

Often I heard Mrs. Bellamy tell about "way back when" they expressed her young sister to relatives in Idaho, or maybe it was Nevada. They put her in the care of the American Express. Shipping instructions were pinned on her dress and the railway crews took her safely to her destination.

The University of Wyoming conferred on Mary G. Bellamy, the honorary degree of Doctor of Laws, in 1952, when she was 91 years of age.

ROY BEST

I HAD SPENT the day in Canon City, Colorado, with six hundred cattlemen and their wives and friends inspecting the prison cell blocks where the men at the Colorado State Penitentiary were housed in clean, light, airy surroundings and where there were canary birds, flowers, and radios. We had visited the bake shop in which one of the inmates had written that plaintive song, "You'll Never Know How Much I Miss You."

We had been banquetted in the dining hall where big placards showed that some twenty prisoners had subscribed for $1,000 Liberty Bonds and many had given blood to the Red Cross Blood Bank. At last we were seated in the big recreation hall facing a small stage.

Warden Roy Best, with his big, battered Stetson hat in one hand, and with his beautiful Doberman at his heels, stepped to the microphone on the platform.

"Ladies and Gentlemen," he began, "I am more than happy to welcome you here--."

Just then a colored boy wearing a cook's snowy white apron and cap tiptoed into the hall and approached the platform where the warden was standing.

"Mistah Warden," he said.

"Dewey," the warden scowled. "You mustn't interrupt—."

"But, Mr. Warden," Dewey persisted. "This is mighty important. It's about dat man dat's been foolin' around my wife--."

"Not now, Dewey. I'll talk to you later," said the warden, frowning.

The audience shifted uneasily.

"But dat man--he's here now. He's right here in dis room--."

You could have heard a pin drop in that big hall.

"Which one is he, Dewey?" The warden was now all attention.

"Dat man right over there." And Dewey pointed an accusing finger towards one of the best-known and most popular cattle buyers in the state of Colorado nicknamed, "Red."

The audience rocked and howled with laughter at the cattle buyer's expense. Dewey retreated with a big grin.

The joke of the warden and Dewey had gone over with a bang. We found out later that this was not the first time the two had put on a similar "act" for the entertainment of guests at the penitentiary.

After our visit I wrote an article and sold it to Editor Shuttleworth of *True Detective Magazine.* He paid me well and thanked me, saying that Roy Best was a "pet" of his.

Not long after that a former Denver detective spoke to the members of my Denver Woman's Press Club, about the writing of crime stories.

He said we should not expect to sell stories about murders and serious crimes in Denver as he and another detective "had the field sewed up."

Shortly after his talk there was a prison break in Canon City. Twelve men escaped. The newspapers were crowded with stories about the escapees and their captures.

Because Warden Roy Best succeeded in capturing all of the escapees and returned them to their cells in rather short order, the *Denver Post* carried his picture in its "Hall of Fame" column.

I cut out the picture and sent the clipping to Editor Shuttleworth with the comment, "Here is your pet, Roy Best, for his quick work after the prison break."

Shuttleworth sent a telegram. "What prison break? I didn't know there was one. If you want the story it is yours."

I bought back issues of the newspapers and traced each escapee until he was captured. I asked Warden Best to sign my story "As told by Warden Best." I told him I would split the proceeds with him. I split the fine check from *True Detective* with the warden. Later when I mentioned that I had, Shuttleworth said he had never heard of a public official accepting pay like that. He sent me an additional check!

BLACK KETTLE'S WIDOW

IT WAS A blistering day in early September 1938. The Wyoming Pioneer Association had just reburied the bones of Chief Black Kettle near their Pioneer Cabin in the State Fair Grounds at Douglas, Wyoming.

A Sioux interpreter had obtained consent from Black Kettle's widow to talk to me. I sat down next to the little wizened old Indian woman, on a sagebrush knoll. She wore a calico dress and had a black shawl over her head and shoulders.

Her husband, Chief Black Kettle had been killed in 1903, by a sheriff's posse, while illegally hunting antelope in Wyoming with a band of Sioux friends.

The law forbade hunting in the area where they were and when warned they had refused to return to their reservations.

The interpreter began quietly to tell Mrs. Black Kettle that I wanted to visit with her.

Mrs. Black Kettle's temper matched the heat of that hot, dusty place. Her tone was bitter.

Through the interpreter she said, "The white men murdered my husband. You are all murderers. You stole our land and you killed off all our wild game. They were our food."

What could I say? I tried to tell her that the sheriff warned the hunters to go back to their reservation. Even the white men were not allowed to hunt where the red men were.

But she would not listen and began wailing and moaning and swaying back and forth.

"She is very old and very tired," the interpreter said. I nodded and told her good-bye and left.

NATHANIEL K. BOSWELL

NATHANIEL K. BOSWELL, known all over the Rocky Mountains as the "Border Detective," was simply "Grandpa" Boswell to me when I was growing up in Laramie, Wyoming. He had white hair and a long white beard. He spoke softly and was especially fond of children.

Mr. Boswell's daughter, Minnie Boswell Oviatt, and her husband, Charles, and family were close friends of our Wright family. We visited back and forth.

I loved to go to the Boswell town house. It was a long, many-roomed officers' quarters that had been moved from old Fort Saunders to Fifth and Grand in Laramie.

Our favorite play place in the rambling old structure was the big room filled with stuffed birds and wild animals, fancy woodwork and beautiful antique furniture made at the penitentiary of which N.K. Boswell had, at one time, been warden. I can now see his grandson, five-year-old Clarence Oviatt, riding his stuffed badger, "Jim."

It was not until I began to do research in western history that I realized that "Grandpa" Boswell was famous. He had captured outlaws and even had Jesse James locked up in his jail at one time.

N.K. Boswell had a fine cattle ranch on the Big Laramie River which bordered the Wyoming-Colorado line, southwest of Laramie.

My father, G.L. Wright, built the big barn on the Boswell ranch when we first moved to Wyoming about 1901.

It was on the small bridge over the Laramie River, near the barn, that I caught my first rainbow trout. From then on I was an ardent fisherwoman.

My mother treasured a lilac bush--purple--next to our ranch house on the Little Laramie, which was carried to her on horseback by U.S. Marshal Boswell. It had been taken from a cutting which he had brought from his old home in Vermont. The bush was still blooming when my mother moved from the ranch in 1935.

When my Grandmother Wright was living in Laramie, Mr. Boswell always shared with her maple sugar from a barrel sent to him each winter from Vermont.

"Old Boz," he was called in the early days when he was chasing and capturing outlaws.

"How did you get 'em?" he was once asked, when he brought in five especially dangerous highwaymen whom he captured near Rock Creek.

"I didn't take a brass band with me," was N.K.'s reply.

WALTER BRENNAN

E WERE IN THE domed banquet room of the National Cowboy Hall of Fame in Oklahoma City, Oklahoma, in April 1973.

When dinner was over a motion picture screen was lowered and a brief sketch of Agnes Wright Spring was thrown on the screen. Then the drums began a soft roll. The lights dimmed and the orchestra went into action as I walked alone from my table to the rostrum.

President Joel McCrae of the Hall escorted me up the three or four steps and toward the podium. There, in brilliant spotlight stood Walter Brennan, a trustee of the Hall. He was holding a bronze horseman, the coveted Trustee Award. Clearly he read:

"Western Heritage Wrangler Award
National Cowboy Hall of Fame and Western Heritage Center
Agnes Wright Spring, Historian
Outstanding Contribution
to the Preservation of Western History
Trustee Award, 1973."

When he finished reading, Walter Brennan handed the trophy to me, then kissed me on the cheek.

How I was so naive, I don't know. I was so surprised to be with Walter Brennan in person that I reared back like a young wild colt being roped for the first time. Cameras snapped and caught me with my mouth open. (*The Oklahoma Magazine* printed that picture later!)

I managed to recover and smiled. I thanked the trustees then told the following story about General Patrick Hurley and Will Rogers.

I said when word reached me of the award, I was on Cloud 9. One evening while attending a convention of writers in Santa Fe, Mr. Spring and I were among about 300 guests who were entertained by General and Mrs. Hurley in their beautiful home on a hill near Santa Fe.

My husband and I were late in arriving and the General met us at the door. With two other guests he gathered us into a small circle and put his arms over our shoulders.

"I am going to tell you something," the General said, "I've never told before. Will Rogers was a long-time friend of mine. He brought cattle up the trail for me. When I was sworn in as Secretary of War in Washington, Will was standing next to me. After I took the oath, he whispered something to me. Reporters crowded around and wanted to know what Will had said. We would not tell them. And this is the first time I've told anyone. Will said, 'Don't Get Stuck On Yourself, Big Boy.' "

"I'll try to remember that," I finished.

I still could scarcely realize I had received my award from the hands of Walter Brennan. I had long admired him in motion pictures and T.V.

I later met Mrs. Brennan and their family. There was no question that Walter Brennan was the highlight of the big gathering. There were many celebrities there--Joel McCrae, Barbara Stanwyck, Will Geer, Doctor Green and others--but Walter Brennan always was the center of attention.

He had been elected to the Hall of Fame of Great Picture Performers in 1971, and to the board of trustees of the National Cowboy Hall of Fame in October, 1972.

He passed away in September, 1973.

According to *Persimmon Hill*, "The bond of friendship between Walter Brennan and the Cowboy Hall of Fame was strong."

MRS. J.J. BROWN "UNSINKABLE MOLLY BROWN"

MRS. J.J. BROWN, "The Unsinkable Molly Brown," was so-called because of her bravery during the sinking of the *S.S. Titanic* in 1912. She had married John J. Brown in Leadville, Colorado, who became a millionaire from his mining ventures.

Plays, fiction, stories of all kinds have been written about Molly Brown but I shall attempt here to tell only the things that I know personally about the Brown family.

My husband, Archer T. Spring, a Bostonian, attended the Colorado School of Mines at Golden, Colorado, with Larry Brown, Molly's son.

Years later we met Larry and his second wife in Denver. About 1945 when I was assisting in the Western History Department of the Denver Public Library, Larry Brown came in to do research about his mother. At first he was uncommunicative, but when he found that I was Arch Spring's wife, he placed confidence in me and let me help with the research. He hoped to disprove the various legends which pictured Molly Brown as illiterate, coarse, a social climber. To Larry's satisfaction we found a number of things very much in his mother's favor.

Arch and I had cocktails with the Browns in their apartment and even discussed the possibility of my collaborating with Larry in writing his mother's story. Larry talked freely and told us of the financial difficulties the family had had with Molly Brown in her later years and how they had become estranged. Larry died on April 3, 1949, before we had started any collaboration.

In August, 1949, I was called to a position with the Sacramento Public Library, in Sacramento, California, and did not have time to follow up the Molly Brown story.

After I returned to Colorado in the autumn of 1950, I renewed my acquaintance with Larry's widow. She seemed at first to want me to work with her on a story of Molly Brown. She gave me some scrapbooks, photographs, and two dresses that had belonged to Molly Brown. In fact, I rescued one of the gowns from a barrel where it had been consigned to the Salvation Army pickup.

As often happens with amateur writers, after working on a subject they decide they can write it themselves without outside help. Mrs. Brown decided she would write the book by herself. But she did not do it.

She passed away on October 18, 1956. I immediately got in touch with Lawrence Brown, Jr., who came to Denver from California to take care of his stepmother's estate.

He called me from Mrs. Brown's residence and was overwhelmed with the disposal of the household and personal belongings. I talked to him chiefly about his father's mining papers which were filed in a four or five-drawer steel file. Larry Jr. showed me the blueprints of mines, mining reports and records which had great historical significance, especially in the Leadville area. He told me that he knew his father had hoped someday to reopen some of the mines but that the cost of getting rid of the water in the shafts would be prohibitive. He told me that because of the immense cost, he had no idea of trying to salvage any of the mines. Too, he did not want to move the steel file to California.

I assured him that if these records were placed in the State Historical Society that he could consult them at any time.

After we had talked at length, he asked, "How soon could you get the file?"

"In half an hour," I assured him. Our staff moved the file of the precious mining records into our Society's library.

Before he left for California, Lawrence P. Brown, Jr. told me confidentially, as it had been told to him, why Molly Brown had left his grandfather, J.J. Brown. It is a story that will not be told by me.

STRUTHERS BURT

WHEN I WAS called to Cheyenne, Wyoming to act as editor of the "Wyoming Guide" for the Federal Writers' Project, Dan Greenburg, head of the Wyoming Planning Commission, worked closely with Mark Christensen, the state director of the Writers' Project.

One day Greenburg came into our office after a trip to Jackson Hole where he had met and talked with Struthers Burt, a popular novelist, writer and poet. Mr. Burt was working on a book about northern Wyoming.

"Bundle up your field work and send it to Struthers Burt," Dan advised Mark Christensen. "He'll return it O.K."

At that stage of the game I doubt if Greenburg or Christensen either one thought the "Wyoming Guide" would ever be published. There was a general feeling that the WPA would not last.

So, upon Mr. Christensen's instructions, we bundled up what field work we had and sent it to Mr. Burt, at Jackson, Wyoming.

In due time the material was returned to our office. Shortly afterward Struthers Burt telephoned me from Jackson and asked if I would collaborate with him on a book on Wyoming in general.

Evidently Dan Greenburg had told him of my experience in working with Wyoming history. I declined and told him I was too involved as editor of our project to take up anything else at that time.

Struthers Burt's book called "Powder River," was well received. What more he wrote about Wyoming I do not know.

Among his best-known writings were: "Powder River," "Diary of a Dude Wrangler," which was delightful, and "Philadelphia Holy Experiment."

Struthers Burt died in 1954 at the age of 74, after a long illness.

NICHOLAS MURRAY BUTLER

NE OF MY MOST vivid memories is of President Nicholas Murray Butler of Columbia University standing before the student body on April 7, 1917.

There was absolute silence in the huge gymnasium as hundreds of students, men and women, waited to hear him speak. Without preliminaries President Butler read the Declaration of War by President Woodrow Wilson, against Germany.

"You know what you have to do," President Butler said.

Tears were running down many cheeks as the sober-faced audience moved towards the exits.

For weeks headlines had screamed across the news sheets. The tension was almost unbearable. But now there was silence. We knew what we had to do.

GOLDIE CAMERON

OLDIE CAMERON rode bucking bronchos in Buffalo Bill's Wild West Show. At one time she was a professional wrestler.

When I knew her she was a retired resident of Nederland, Colorado, living with the memories of the exciting life she had lived.

She had accumulated scrapbooks and photographs galore and through the years she had kept in close touch with 175 rodeo riders and performers.

She delighted to tell that on horseback, she married a champion broncho rider in Madison Square Garden, New York City before an audience of 8,000.

As I recall it, she had broken her leg in a wild ride, but she did not delay the wedding. She mounted her horse with a cast on one leg and went through with the ceremony as scheduled.

Maurice Frink, executive director of the State Historical Society asked me to take part in a program with Goldie. I was to tell about my little brochure called "Buffalo Bill and His Horses." Goldie was to tell of her experiences with the Wild West Show.

Goldie had a front tooth missing but that did not embarrass her in the least. She greeted the audience with a broad smile and held her listeners fascinated while she related some of her most exciting experiences. She concluded with details of how she was the only person allowed to go and come when Bonfils and Tammen impounded Buffalo Bill's show in the old Overland Park grounds in Denver.

"I drove the water wagon," Goldie explained. "And the guards had to let me in and out."

Goldie agreed to do a story of her life with me, but about that time the state highway department decided to build a new road through Nederland across Goldie's property and she wrote me that her house was to be moved and that she had put her scrapbooks and photographs and letters into storage. We lost touch.

JANE CANARY - CALAMITY JANE

I CAN CLAIM no close touch with Calamity Jane but I have walked in her shadow many times. I have talked with persons who saw her and knew her.

Earnest A. Logan, my good friend in Cheyenne, told me he had seen Calamity and her pal, Soldier Kate, several times at the local theater and also on the old Black Hills Trail when she was driving a bull team, bullwhacking on the old Deadwood Trail.

Mrs. T.J. Cahill, whose husband was a bailiff or jailer, told me that one time when Calamity had been arrested for driving a team away from Fort Laramie without permission, she was on trial in Cheyenne. Mrs. Cahill loaned her a good dress to wear to court.

After Calamity was out of jail she paraded up and down the streets of Cheyenne in the borrowed dress, much to Mrs. Cahill's dismay.

I received a letter from a Mrs. Robinson, then living in Nebraska, who replied to my question about Calamity's funeral in 1903.

"Yes," replied Mrs. Robinson, "I did play the organ at Calamity Jane's funeral, but there was nothing out of the ordinary about it. Just the regular funeral for an old-timer."

A legislator from Hot Springs County, Wyoming, whom I knew, told me that he had been one of the pall bearers at Calamity's funeral.

"We thought it would be a good joke to bury her next to Wild Bill Hickok because Bill would have turned over in his grave if he had known it."

"But Wild Bill knew her?" I asked.

"Sure, he met her in bars which she frequented but Wild Bill was not a lover of Calamity. John Hunton vouched for the fact that she was one of the occupants of the Hog Ranch at one time."

Mrs. X. of Newcastle, who had a little store on the old trail, said she had sold dress goods--yard goods to Calamity and that Jane liked fancy clothes, as well as the man's garb she usually wore.

JOSEPH "JOSIE" M. CAREY
LOUISA M.D. CAREY

WHEN I graduated from the University of Wyoming in June, 1913, and went to Cheyenne to become Assistant State Librarian in the Supreme Court Library, it was my good fortune to be included among the young women who were close friends of the Carey family. My boss, Frances Davis of Buffalo, Wyoming, was a distant relative of Joseph "Josie" M. Carey, and the Jones twins, Emily and Evelyn, were particular favorites of Governor Joseph M. and Mrs. Carey. We were invited often to the Carey home and assisted at receptions and parties.

Joseph M. Carey, a graduate in law from the University of Pennsylvania, came to Wyoming in 1869. He had served as mayor of Cheyenne, U.S. Senator from Wyoming, and in his later years, became governor of Wyoming in 1911.

Historians and writers usually stress only his political career as a competitor of Senator Francis E. Warren.

I knew Joseph M. Carey as a kindly, jovial friend, a strong advocate of equal rights. He was always interested in the work of young people and when he was governor assisted women who needed work in finding positions with the state.

I was eager to learn all of the early history of Wyoming that I could, and Governor Carey seemed to enjoy telling me many incidents about early days in Cheyenne.

When I heard him tell a high school graduating class that some Wyoming girl or boy should write the story of Caspar Collins, hero of the Platte Bridge Fight in 1866, I told him I would like to write the story.

It was Governor Carey who put me in touch with John Friend of Rawlins, and Julius Mayer of Denver, comrades of Caspar Collins in the 11th Ohio Volunteer Cavalry. I met other comrades when I visited Caspar's home in Hillsboro, Ohio.

One Halloween Frances Davis, Evelyn Jones and I decided to decorate the statue of a soldier in front of the Capitol. It was a stone replica of a Spanish American War soldier taking the oath of induction. It was not considered a very outstanding piece of statuary. Because the soldier's right hand was raised for taking the oath, folks in Cheyenne dubbed the statue, "Old Never Again."

We three girls decided to hang a bottle of milk on the upraised hand. How we managed to put a stocking cap on the statue's head and drape the body with a large flowered quilt lining, I don't know. But we did. As I recall, the statue had been paid for by the Woman's Relief Corps.

We went to our offices in the Capitol the next morning with innocent-looking faces. Very shortly we were summoned to appear in the governor's office. Governor Joseph M. Carey was sitting at his desk.

"Young ladies," he began. "Members of the Women's Relief Corps are in the building," he paused, "selling tickets for a benefit dinner. I would appreciate it if you all would buy tickets. Thank you."

There was a twinkle in his eyes as we filed out of the office without a word.

The statue later was moved to another location.

When in the summer of 1916, I was notified that I had been awarded a $500.00 Fellowship by Pi Beta Phi, to study journalism at the Pulitzer School of Journalism in Columbia University, New York City, I went to talk to Ex-Governor Carey. I asked if I could borrow $500.00 as I would need at least $1,000 to go to Columbia. The Governor said he would like to think it over and for me to come back the next day.

When I returned to his office, he said he did not like to think of me obligating myself for the $500.00. It would be too hard to pay back. He paused. "But," he continued, "I have $500.00 here for you which is not to be returned. There will be no strings attached. I can't tell you where it came from."

Dr. Grace Hebard may have contributed part of the amount, but I think it all came from Governor Carey himself.

Mrs. Thomas, wife of Bishop Nathaniel S. Thomas, gave me $100.00. I had been doing some work for the Bishop "after hours," transcribing the letters from a dictaphone. Governor John B. Kendrick, who had become governor in 1915, granted me a leave of absence.

When my Caspar Collins book was published in 1927 by Columbia University Press, I dedicated it to Governor Joseph M. Carey.

Some years later I applied to the graduate school of the University of Wyoming for a master's degree, with Joseph M. Carey as the subject for my thesis. My application was approved, but the Depression made it necessary for me to accept a position instead of doing the graduate work.

Mrs. Louisa M. Carey, the governor's wife, was a real character. She had come to Cheyenne from Dubuque, Iowa, with her father David, who was Surveyor General of the Territory. For many years she and "Josie," her favorite name for her husband, were the social leaders of Cheyenne. Their home was a three-story mansion, said to have been built for Mrs. Carey by her husband when she became restless and was going to take their two small sons to California. He promised that if she would stay he would build the biggest and best house in Cheyenne. He did. The home was luxuriously furnished with Oriental rugs, lace curtains, and beautiful furniture.

As a hostess, Mrs. Carey was unexcelled. Her dining table, with its centerpiece of red roses, glittered with crystal and silver. V.I.P.'s, legislators, big cattlemen, and important visitors enjoyed the Carey hospitality.

I remember well seeing Harry Lauder, as a guest, in his plaid kilts and carrying his crooked walking stick. Of course he sang "A-Roamin' in the Gloamin' " and other songs. In her usual frank way, Mrs. Carey said to me that Harry Lauder "was rude." More likely she meant crude.

Although Mrs. Carey was an Episcopalian and was an ardent supporter of Bishop Nathaniel S. Thomas, an Episcopalian, her favorite dinner guest was the Catholic Bishop Patrick A. McGovern, who was a delightful storyteller.

In speaking of Bishop McGovern I am reminded of a call I made at his home. He had written a history of the Catholic church in Wyoming over which he presided. I wrote from Fort Collins to ask if I might obtain a copy of his book. He wrote that he would be glad to give me a copy if I would drop by his home on my next visit to Cheyenne.

My husband took me to the Bishop's home and waited outside in our car. Fifteen minutes later when I appeared with the autographed copy of the book, my husband asked what the Bishop and I talked about.

To his amazement I said, "Our gall bladders." The Bishop was recovering from a recent gall bladder operation.

Louisa M. Carey was always high-spirited and demanding. And above all, outspoken. When I first went to Cheyenne as Assistant State Librarian Historian, I went to call on Mrs. Carey, the governor's wife. I had had my shoes dyed brown to match my suit.

It was a warm afternoon and as we sat in the Carey drawing room, I smelled a strong odor of shoe dye.

"Mrs. Carey," I said. "Does the smell of the shoe polish bother you?"

"Oh, my dear," she exclaimed. "I just had my shoes dyed yesterday!"

We laughed when I explained. It was on that first visit that she said: "Take off the high collar. It's too hot to wear anything like that."

Mrs. Carey became a good friend and now and then when the Governor was away she would send for me or one of the Jones twins to talk to her.

Mrs. Carey was exceedingly proud of having been the wife of a Wyoming Governor and U.S. Senator and the mother of a Wyoming Governor and U.S. Senator. Her son, Robert D. Carey, became Governor in 1919, and U.S. Senator in 1930.

Governor Robert D. Carey invited me to lead the Grand March with him at the Inaugural Ball as Julia, his wife, was, I think, in Europe at the time. He reappointed me as State Librarian and State Historian, ex-officio. Julia Carey was the daughter of General Freeman and was as high-spirited as her mother-in-law, Louisa Carey. I was in touch with Julia for a number of years. She loved to spend time in Jackson Hole and I recall one Christmas card which she sent was of Santa Claus fishing in Jackson Lake.

The Jones twins and I often were guests in the home of Charles and Nellie Carey, the younger Carey son. When I went to Columbia University on a leave of absence, Charlie and Nellie gave me a beautiful leather traveling case.

J.M. Carey and Brother were among the earliest cattlemen in the Wyoming Territory. On assignment, I wrote for Don Ornduff, editor of the *American Hereford Journal*, an article about The Meadows and Careyhurst, the Carey ranches, and the story of their fine Hereford cattle.

I was stunned and deeply grieved on the morning of January 17, 1937 to receive a call from the office of the Wyoming Stock Growers Association telling me that Robert D. Carey had died of a heart attack upon his return to Cheyenne after attending a livestock convention in Texas. I was asked to prepare a memorial for publication in the Association's *Cow Country* publication.

I admired Robert Carey as much as I did his father, Joseph M. Both were fine executives and men.

When Woodrow Wilson was on his last speaking tour, I went with the Careys to hear him. After the meeting I heard Joseph M. and Robert discussing President Wilson. Instead of talking politics they were agreeing that President Wilson was the best-dressed man they had seen in ages!

JOHN B. KENDRICK

IN JANUARY 1, 1915, a Democrat, a one-time Texas cowboy, then a millionaire cattleman of Sheridan, Wyoming, succeeded Joseph M. Carey as governor of Wyoming. His name was John B. Kendrick.

The Kendricks had two children: Rosa and Manville. They moved into the governor's mansion in Cheyenne and were especially popular with the younger set.

My boss, Frances Davis, was a long-time friend of the Kendricks and despite our Republican affiliations we continued to hold office in the State Library.

We enjoyed dinners and parties at the mansion and eagerly listened while Governor Kendrick told about some of his early experiences. He had brought longhorns up the Texas Trail for a man named Wulfjen. He later married Ula Wulfjen, daughter of his employer. Now and then he reminisced about darning his own socks and performing domestic duties while on the range in Wyoming. He did not deny the story about how he and a companion once roped a mountain lion.

In April, 1973, my dinner partner at the banquet in the National Cowboy Hall of Fame was Manville Kendrick of Wyoming, a trustee of the Hall.

FRANK L. HOUX

IN FEBRUARY 1917, John B. Kendrick went to Washington as U.S. Senator from Wyoming. Frank L. Houx, Secretary of State, took over as acting governor. He was called "Tin Horn Frank," affectionately by his friends. He wore cutaway coats, striped trousers and bright red ties. I liked Governor Houx. He was a pioneer of Cody, Wyoming. He was a Democrat, an old-line politician, and he knew how to play the game.

Some time after Governor Houx took over the governor's office, I received an offer of a position in New York City at $65.00 a week to do publicity work for a big religious concern. The offer came through the School of Journalism. The salary in those days was most attractive. It was quite an increase over the salary I was getting.

When I told Miss Davis about the offer and that I might resign, she said she was thinking seriously of marrying Mart Tisdale, a rancher of Buffalo, in a few months, and asked me to stay. She said she would talk to Governor Houx about it.

Then Frances told me that Mart Tisdale's father was shot to death in 1891 when he was on his way home to his small Johnson County ranch, taking Christmas presents for his children. It was really the beginning of the so-called "Johnson County War," a fight between the big cattle owners and the rustlers and homesteaders.

Frances (Dolly) was the daughter of Henry Winter (Hard Winter) Davis who owned a ranch at Sussex in Johnson County. He threatened to disown Dolly if she married Mart Tisdale.

A wealthy uncle in the East had educated Frances at a young woman's finishing school in New York City. She was attractive and dressed exceptionally well. She had several suitors in Cheyenne and as the months slipped by her plans to marry Mart seemed to grow dim. I had little hope of succeeding to her position as State Librarian.

But one night about midnight in November or December 1917, there was a loud knock at my little apartment door.

"Get your bag packed," Frances said. "We are leaving for Omaha. Mart is shipping cattle and I have decided to marry him. We want you to stand up with us."

There was a real Wyoming blizzard on. But we made our way through the snow and wind to the Union Pacific depot. There we went aboard a special Pullman which had been arranged for livestock men shipping to Omaha. Frances' brother, Mark Davis, already was aboard.

The Pullman was attached to the long string of cattle cars and we were on our way. Traffic along the line was sidetracked in the blizzard to let the livestock train go by.

We registered at the Lafayette Hotel in Omaha and made a few plans for the wedding. It was 18 degrees below zero about nine o'clock in the morning when we reached the Episcopalian Cathedral and found a minister waiting. As the bride said, "I will" or "I do" her breath spiraled up in frost. Mark Davis and I were the only witnesses.

As soon as we could get back downtown we had a good, hot wedding breakfast. Then the bridegroom, Mart, said, "Come on girls, we're heading for the stockyards."

I cannot recall ever having been as cold as we were walking along the narrow walkways on top of the pens looking down on the cattle.

Before Mark and I left to return to Wyoming, Frances assured me that Governor Houx would appoint me as State Librarian and State Historian, ex-officio, to succeed her. We returned on a regular Union Pacific passenger train.

Governor Houx kept his word and appointed me, a Republican, despite the pressure which Attorney General Douglas Preston tried to bring against me.

"Tin Horn Frank" was succeeded as governor by Robert D. Carey, a son of Joseph M. on January 6, 1919, under whose administration I served until I resigned to be married to Archer T. Spring on February 14, 1921.

The last time I saw Governor Houx was in the late 1930's. He was retired and living at the Irma Hotel in Cody, his home town! He seemed glad to see me.

It was while he was in the Capitol that his son, Christy, was drowned in Lindenmeir Lake near Fort Collins while ice boating.

BILL CARLISLE

ANY STORIES and an autobiography have been published about Bill Carlisle, so-called "The last of the Union Pacific train robbers."

In his later years Bill married a nurse and owned a filling station and a motel in Laramie where we bought gas and chatted with him. He was a well-liked citizen. My reason for including him here is that Warden Alonzo Roach of the Wyoming State Penitentiary, dictated to me the story of the capture of Bill after his escape from the penitentiary.

Among other things the warden said was that after he shot and wounded Carlisle, they took him to the hospital in Douglas, Wyoming. Some of the women of the town tried to make a hero of Bill. They sent him flowers and gifts. One of the nurses turned on Warden Roach and said, "I wish you had been the one who got shot instead of Carlisle."

I had dinner with Warden and Mrs. Roach in their home at the penitentiary in Rawlins. A powerful black man served the dinner of roast elk meat. When he left the dining room I asked the warden why he was "in."

The warden said, "Murder."

"Isn't Mrs. Roach afraid to have him working around the house?" I came back.

"No," answered the warden. "He wouldn't hurt anyone. He murdered his *wife.*"

I met and talked with Bill Carlisle in his later years when we bought gasoline for our car at his filling station. He also owned a motel. He had married a nurse in Kemmerer, Wyoming and finished his life as a respected, industrious citizen.

KIT CARSON III

ROBABLY one of the best-known names in the history of the Old West is that of Kit Carson.

I knew his grandson, Kit Carson III, who lived in Alamosa, Colorado. I enjoyed his visits to my office in the State Museum in Denver. One day Kenny Englert, one of our loyal Society members, stopped by my office with Kit III, who proudly showed me his ticket to the National Western Stock Show and Rodeo that afternoon. I examined the ticket and noted the seat number.

After my visitors had gone, I called up the announcer at the show and told him they were going to have a distinguished visitor. I gave him the seat number. The announcer followed through and introduced Kit Carson III to a cheering audience of many hundreds.

I treasure the fine snapshot of himself which Kit III gave me.

A great-granddaughter of Kit Carson I, who worked at Neustetter's in Denver, always came to the celebration held on Colorado Day around the fountain at Colfax and Broadway. During the ceremony a fireman scaled a ladder and placed a large wreath of flowers at the foot of the statue of Kit Carson on horseback. It seems that many years before when it was decided to erect a fountain with a statue at the location, the sculptor planned the figure of an Indian to be placed above the fountain. The Pioneer Men and Women objected strenuously and a bronze equestrian statue of Kit Carson won the day.

BUTCH CASSIDY

I AM ONE WHO never believed the story that Butch Cassidy was killed in South America. I had long had much of the information which Butch's sister, Mrs. Betenson, used in her recent book.

Old-timers near Lander declared he was around there about the 1930's. Josie Bassett, an old flame of Butch's, said he had come to see her. And as far back as 1940 one or two persons had told me Butch became a businessman in Spokane, Washington, under another name.

My interest in Butch Cassidy began when I was State Librarian-State Historian of Wyoming. Attorney General "Doug" Preston used to come into my office and tell me about going out on the Red Desert, south of Green River, to meet Butch to arrange to protect him legally, after a bank holdup. "Doug" was his lawyer. Their meeting place was not far from Brown's Hole.

Jim Calverly, who lived in Cheyenne when I did, told me that his father, an officer, captured Butch and took him into custody before he was sent to the penitentiary.

Andrew Manseau, an elderly pioneer, whom I interviewed at Burris, Wyoming, near Dubois, knew Butch well and sold bluestem hay to him for horses. Butch often stayed at Manseau's ranch and his gang came back and forth when they were stealing horses in Dakota and trailing them through Jackson Hole to sell them in Utah. Then they would steal horses in Utah and take them to Dakota to sell.

Mart Christensen, newspaperman, who had seen Butch and his gang in Powder Springs years before, told me that he talked with a man in Lander who had taken Butch into the mountains in the 1930's near there, supposedly on a prospecting trip. But the man thought Butch was looking for a hidden cache.

The Sundance Kid, whose name is linked with that of Butch Cassidy was a frequent visitor in Johnson County, Wyoming. Genevra Brock, who grew up on a ranch near Buffalo, told me that the Sundance Kid used to come to the Brock ranch when she was a child and he brought blue hair ribbons to her.

And so it went in Wyoming in the early 1900's--history at every turn.

CARRIE CHAPMAN CATT

ARRIE CHAPMAN CATT, national leader in the woman suffrage movement, was a classmate of Dr. Grace Raymond Hebard at the University of Iowa in the early 1880's and was a close friend.

At the time of Mrs. Catt's first visit to Laramie, about 1912, I was assistant to librarian Hebard, who asked me to meet Mrs. Catt at the train and escort her to Dr. Hebard's home, the Doctor's Inn. I met the train with Mr. Howard's team and hack and found Mrs. Catt very cordial. She was a striking looking woman, beautifully dressed.

In the autumn of 1916 when I went to Columbia University I met Mrs.Catt's niece, Ruhe Lynn of Walsenberg, Colorado. She was living in Whittier Hall where I resided. We became good friends.

In December, Mrs. Walter McNabb Miller, an official of the New York equal suffrage movement and a close friend of Mrs. Catt, employed Ruhe and me to do some vacation work. We were to canvass big apartment houses to try to obtain names of women who wanted to vote. New York then did not have equal rights.

We were paid by the hour. We would go to a big apartment house and select a buzzer on a top floor. If the owner buzzed the door so we could get in we would then work our way up through the apartment house.

Some doors would be slammed in our faces at the words "Equal Rights."

When we asked one woman if she would like to vote, she stomped her foot and said, "I hope you never get the vote!" We smiled and said, "We have the vote. We are from Colorado and Wyoming."

We had such difficulty in getting doors opened if we mentioned we were from the Equal Suffrage Association, that we changed our tactics and said we were "two young women from Columbia University."

Those were magic words and doors opened.

We did succeed in getting a large number of names on our petition. And we hoped we had helped the "cause."

Mrs. Catt invited us to have Christmas dinner with Miss Hayes and herself in her Park Avenue apartment.

Ruhe and I walked down from Whittier Hall at Columbia University. We went through Central Park and the only unusual incident of our walk was a warning from a mounted policeman to get off the equestrian pathway. He was riding a beautiful horse.

Mrs. Catt took us in her car, with her chaffeur, to the theatre to see Mary Roberts Rhinehart's "The Bat." I still can see the dagger in the ceiling picked out by a brilliant spotlight!

Back at the apartment, which was luxuriously furnished, we had a delicious dinner, with a tiny Christmas tree in the center of the table. Each one of us had a fancy paper cap and received gifts.

Mrs. Catt and Miss Hayes were delightful hostesses. It was my first Christmas so far from Wyoming.

In June, 1921, I was happy to renew my friendship with Mrs. Catt when the University of Wyoming gave her an honorary degree. I think this was the first one granted by the University. Dr. Hebard entertained her at a tea in her garden for Mrs. Catt.

WILLIAM F. CODY - BUFFALO BILL

I SAW William F. (Buffalo Bill) Cody only once. He was mounted on a spirited horse and was leading the parade of his Wild West Show. His manager had sent tickets to my mother, who was postmistress of our ranch post office at Filmore, Wyoming.

To me Buffalo Bill was and always will be the greatest showman of the Old West.

Grant Vincent, my Uncle Ed Vincent's brother, rode with the Wild West Show. Ed Vincent had married my mother's youngest sister, Robekah Dorsett Findley Vincent.

Grant wrote letters to his family on letterhead of the Wild West Show when he was in Europe. He told many interesting things about his fellow riders and the Indians. In England he broke one leg while riding a broncho to the show.

When the "epizootic" struck and killed many of the show's horses in mid-Europe, Cody sent Grant back to the States to buy horses for replacements. Grant bought horses in the Fort Collins, Colorado area, freighted them to New York and then took a boat-load to Italy where he rejoined the show.

Buffalo Bill's horses always fascinated me and I did considerable research on them. I was especially interested in the painting of him which Rosa Bonheur did while visiting his camp. Later she had a cow pony shipped from Wyoming to her estate in France for study.

Jim White, editor of the *Nebraska Farmer*, asked me to write an article about Buffalo Bill and his horses. I did and he published it in his magazine.

Later, with his permission, I had the article reprinted in a small booklet. Not long after it appeared, I received a letter from William E. Coe, wealthy eastern benefactor of the Coe Library at Yale. Mr. Coe said that the picture of Buffalo Bill which I had credited to a painting by Rosa Bonheur was not the one she painted. He told me he owned the original painting by Bonheur and sent me a photograph of it for which I was grateful. In his picture, Cody was a young man with dark hair. The one I had used showed Cody with white hair and a white goatee. I did some concentrated thinking. I recalled that Robert Lindneux, a skilled Denver artist, had told me about helping with an exhibition of Cody's paintings and posters for one of Denver's big stores. The next time Lindneux came into my office I asked him if he had painted the picture of Buffalo Bill in his later years. He smiled and said he had.

"Why was Rosa Bonheur's name on it?" I wanted to know.

Lindneux's answer was vague, something to the effect that he had neglected to remove it. At any rate, thanks to Mr. Coe, I reprinted my brochure of "Buffalo Bill and His Horses" with the correct photograph of the Bonheur painting.

At the time of Buffalo Bill's death, January 10, 1917, I was at school in New York City. But many years later I learned about his burial from curator Edgar McMechen.

When I was called to the State Historical Society to serve a year as acting historian, my office on the main floor of the museum was only a few steps away from that of Edgar McMechen, curator, who was handling the executive work of the State Historical Society. He knew I was deeply interested in Colorado history and stopped by often to chat. Mac had been editor of *Municipal Facts*, a fine magazine devoted to Denver's civic affairs. He had held a number of responsible positions and was familiar with the politics of Denver. He was familiar with all of the angles.

One afternoon he came into my office, walked to the large window which faced on Fourteenth Avenue, put his foot on the low radiator beneath the window, and gazing out at the Capitol across the street, began talking. His voice sounded almost as if he were talking to himself.

"I had a lot to do with the burial of Buffalo Bill," he said. "The *Denver Post* wanted to keep his body in the Denver area when he died. It was thought that the people of Cody, Wyoming would try to get it. I was asked to negotiate with Mrs. Louisa Cody to have her husband buried in the Lookout Mountain area. I paid her $10,000."

Then he explained that the funeral arrangements were put in the hands of the Elks Club, that Cody's body lay in state in the Capitol, and that there was a big parade with all the fanfare that this great showman deserved.

Mac also explained that railway rails were placed on top of Cody's grave, embedded in four or five feet of concrete to guard against vandals.

I have heard it said many times that Buffalo Bill wanted to be buried on Cedar Mountain near Cody. What few persons know is that about 1903, Buffalo Bill had had a will drawn up by two eminent lawyers of New York City, in which he stated that he wished to be buried in Colorado on a mountain overlooking Denver. A copy of that will, I was told by a most reliable Wyoming gentleman, was on file in a county office in Cody. Later--some years later--Cody made another will in which he named his wife, Louisa, as his heir. I obtained a copy of that second will, but when I asked for a copy of the New York will, I was informed it was not on file, as I had been told.

A postal card in color was published some years back showing a proposed monument with Buffalo Bill on horseback on Lookout Mountain. Money was supposed to be raised for the monument by contributions from school children. Nothing apparently came of the proposal.

But a very fine monument, sculptured by Gertrude Vanderbilt Whitney was built and stands near the town of Cody, Wyoming. While living in Willits, California, from 1970 to 1976, I often talked with Don Coleman, champion rodeo rider, and well-known Hollywood actor, who posed for that Cody, Wyoming, statue.

Don Coleman, born in Sheridan, Wyoming, grew up on a ranch in Montana. At the age of 14 he hit the rodeo circuit as a broncho busting cowboy. He became World Champion Broncho Buster. He appeared in most of the "western" motion pictures in Hollywood and was a good friend of Tim McCoy, whom I had known for years.

Gertrude Vanderbilt Whitney saw pictures of Coleman and asked him to come to New York to pose for the statue of Buffalo Bill, which she had been commissioned to sculpt, to be set up at the entrance to Yellowstone National Park.

Don Coleman was very handsome (and still is) and while he was in New York City was asked to pose for a number of Arrow Collar advertisements. To name all of the motion pictures in which he played would require several pages. One of his greatest feats was training 1400 mules and horses for "Beau Geste", filmed in Yuma, Arizona, with Ronald Coleman and Wallace Beery. He retired in 1934.

Don and his wife, Patricia, whom he married in 1927, live quietly on a 40-acre ranch in the valley adjoining Willits, not far from the big redwoods.

Don still keeps an interest in rodeos. He feeds cattle in good grass years. The Colemans have a collection of Jesse James memorabilia, assembled by Patricia's father, a railway executive.

DANE COOLIDGE

ANE COOLIDGE, nationally-known writer, came to my office when I was director of the "Wyoming Guide" of the Wyoming Writers' Project.

Coolidge had been in northern Wyoming trying to gather data for a book on the Johnson County War. Born in Natick, Massachusetts, in 1877, Dane Coolidge was now living in California. I had read some of his stories in the *Saturday Evening Post* and *Collier's.*

We visited for more than an hour and I let him see what material we had on hand. I told him that I had worked for the daughter of "Hard Winter" Davis, who had married Mart Tisdale--names familiar to anyone studying the "Invasion."

When Dane Coolidge rose to leave he thanked me for my help and then said, "Imagine working with such marvelous material--and being paid for it!"

Mr. Coolidge's visit to my office was in 1938. He died in 1940. If he ever wrote the story of the Johnson County War, I failed to see a copy.

GRACE COOLIDGE

RACE COOLIDGE, wife of President Calvin Coolidge, was a classmate and close friend of Anna Robinson Nickerson, who was on the grand council of Pi Beta Phi, when I was on the council as editor of *The Arrow.*

A small group of friends of Grace Coolidge started a round robin when they graduated from college and faithfully carried on during the years.

Anna Nickerson shared the letters with me. Even though Grace Coolidge was the First Lady, living in the White House, she never failed to add her letter to the robin.

One of Mrs. Coolidge's letters stands out in my memory. It was written after the death of her son, Calvin Jr. She spoke of her great loss and said, "When Calvin was teaching me to swim he always said, 'Keep your chin up, Mother, keep your chin up.' I'm trying to do that."

Anna Nickerson supervised, with the help of our council, the painting of a portrait of Grace Coolidge by Howard Chandler

Christy. For the painting Mrs. Coolidge wore a beautiful red velvet gown and had a white wolfhound at her side. Pi Beta Phi presented the painting to the White House.

Mrs. Coolidge sent portraits of herself and the President for me to use in *The Arrow* and invited me to visit the White House if I came to Washington. She was a very warm person and an understanding one. She had taught in a school for the blind before her marriage to Calvin Coolidge.

JANE COWL

IN THE SPRING of 1917, just after World War I was declared, Jane Cowl was starring on Broadway in "Lilac Time." The story was about two young lovers who were planning to be married but were suddenly separated when the man was sent overseas with the troops.

The play ended on a high note with the heroine, Jane Cowl, waving a small bootie in the air and sobbing, "This is my cross of war."

Tears streamed down many faces as the audience filed out of the theater.

I remarked to my escort that such an ending would not stand up. People were too upset by the war to accept it. Later when I saw "Lilac Time," the ending had been changed.

About thirty years later I saw Jane Cowl in a TV interview. I wrote a note to her telling her I had attended the opening night of "Lilac Time." She wrote a delightful note to me in acknowledgement.

Miss Cowl, who authored or co-authored nine plays, starred in "Smiling Through," and others. "Within the Law" probably was her greatest hit.

Born in Boston, she died in Santa Monica, California, in June 1950, at the age of 65.

HOMER CROY

HOMER CROY's first novel entitled "West of the Water Tower," created a small sensation because of the sex angle. He became a well-established writer through the years.

My first contact with Homer Croy was in doing some research for him when he was writing "The Lady From Colorado." His story was based on the life of Baby Doe Tabor. His book was produced in a play in Central City during the Gold Rush Centennial, 1959.

When Homer Croy asked me for suggestions for another novel, I mentioned "Little Joe" Monoghan, but he was not interested. Then I wrote and asked if he would care to collaborate on the story of "Colorado Charley Utter, Wild Bill's Pard".

Homer Croy wrote back as follows:

Agnes:

I rather favor la idea. I am in the middle of a novel, but I reckon this could be put on the back of the stove. I would come out there and we would talk solemnly about the idea, and as intelligently as we could.

'Pears to me the valuable part is establishing him as the partner of Wild Bill Hickok. Possible title:

WILD BILL HICKOK'S PARDNER
COLORADO CHARLIE.

Is his burial place known? You say he went to heaven from a place in Mexico--quite a long trip, n'est ce pas? (Do you mean New Mexico?)

Could we sell it to *The S.E. Post?*

Pictures?

Are you committed to a publisher?

I've just sold the Jesse James book to Dell, reprint. But I been havin' bad luck with *The Lady From Colorado.* Have been kept from a Broadway production by *The Unsinkable Mrs. Brown.* There is now a bit of talk about doing it come 1960 in Central City, but the theater shoals are so deep & treacherous that I am not as yet putting the money in the bank.

I'll write vous in a jour or deux.

Croy, the Man All Women Fear

(signed H.C.)

When Mr. Croy came through Denver on his way to Central City for the premiere of "The Lady From Colorado," my husband and I met him at the American Legion in Denver and had a nice chat. As I recall it he did not have a cocktail. He seemed very interested in "Colorado Charley."

Now Homer Croy had long had a habit of decorating postal cards or envelopes or letters with unique stamps, headlines from papers, or useless foreign stamps. In fact he laughed and told us that the postal authorities had reprimanded him for the habit.

After he returned home and before we had begun collaboration on "Colorado Charley," Croy sent me a letter addressed in care of the Western History Department of the Denver Public Library, on which he had pasted an advertisement of an infant in diapers crawling on all fours. Under the picture he had written: "This is Agnes Wright Spring at the age of eight months."

My husband, a Bostonian, and not given to practical joking, was furious. He put his foot down and said, "No collaboration with Homer Croy." And that is why I wrote "Colorado Charley: Wild Bill's Pard," on my own.

The following lines sent to me by "H.C." are well worth repeating here:

"To live content with small means, to seek elegance rather than luxury, and refinement rather than fashion; to be worthy not respectable, and wealthy not rich; to study hard, think quietly, talk gently, act frankly; to listen to stars and birds, to babes and sages with open heart; to bear all cheerfully, do all bravely; await occasion, hurry never; in a word, to let the spiritual unbidden and unconscious grow up through the common. This is to be my symphony."

Wm. Henry Channing

"We do not have to live but one day at a time but we are living for eternity in that one day.

"Live, live today, tomorrow never yet on any human being rose or set."

GENERAL GEORGE CUSTER

I HAVE NEVER been a student of Custer and the so-called "Custer Massacre," so can claim little intimate knowledge of General George Custer. In passing, however, I must refer to Robert Hall, Fremont County, Wyoming, rancher and legislator whom I interviewed at his ranch home about 1939.

Robert Hall told me that he was a telegrapher at old Camp Stambaugh near South Pass in 1876.

One morning a runner came in over the mountains with word of the Custer battle. Hall rushed to his telegraph instrument only to find that the wires had been cut.

He saddled his horse, took his instrument and some tools with him and rode along the telegraph line until he could repair it and send a message. He telegraphed to army headquarters in Omaha, telling of the battle.

"It was several days," he said, "before the news was made public."

Why, he did not know.

He has always felt that he sent the first telegraphic message to Omaha headquarters of the great tragedy.

Fremont County has honored Robert Hall and in a parade about 1940 had a float upon which Robert Hall, his horse and his telegraph instrument were featured.

As we concluded our talk, I saw my husband turn pale and he rose to go.

After we had reached our car I asked if he were sick.

"No," he said. "A big bull snake crawled under your chair and I knew if you saw it you might jump off the porch and break your leg."

That was an understatement!

WILLIAM C. DEMING

IN MARCH 1923, William C. Deming, owner and editor of the *Wyoming Tribune*, Cheyenne, Wyoming, was appointed to the U.S. Civil Service Commission in Washington, D.C. by President Warren Harding. Mr. Deming became president of the Commission and was continued in office by Presidents Coolidge and Hoover.

When I first went to Cheyenne to work in the State Library, I called at Mr. Deming's office to ask for advice on how to become a journalist. He told me to try to go to a good school of journalism. He said there were good ones at the University of Wisconsin and at the University of Missouri. But to his mind, the best was the Pulitzer School of Journalism at Columbia University in New York City.

I told him I could not afford to go to one of the schools now, but would start planning.

The next day Mr. Deming telephoned me and asked if I would like to do the society page of the *Wyoming Tribune*! It would be night work and extra hours work, as I had a full-time job in the Capitol. But I said I'd try it.

I interviewed brides, dropped into lectures, looked over tables decorated for formal dinners, consulted with hostesses and arranged to have photographs taken of social events.

I worked hard for about two months, but I didn't like any part of the society reporting. I decided to bow out.

When I told Mr. Deming that I was giving up the society page, he asked how I would like to start a woman's page in the *Wyoming Stockman-Farmer*, which he owned. I was delighted. I started the page with a folksy poem, then a bit of philosophy, then a few features of special interest to ranch and farm women. Of course, there were some recipes, and I had a children's corner with puzzles and little prizes. Among my "fans" were some of the men from isolated ranches or homesteads. One wanted to know the best brand of coffee, one would like a good recipe for gingerbread.

I wrote the women's page and many, many feature articles for twenty-seven years, missing only one copy, despite two major operations in hospitals.

After I moved to Colorado, I sent my copy to Cheyenne by mail to Editor John Charles Thompson, a splendid man and an exceptionally fine journalist. Mr. Thompson gave me free rein on my page. The monetary compensation was small but the experience was invaluable.

Mr. Deming asked me to write his biography, which I began in Cheyenne, and completed in Denver. It was published in 1944 by the Arthur H. Clark Company of Glendale, California. It was a bulky book which grew under Mr. Deming's supervision. He wanted to include about everything.

While the book was in preparation he asked me to interview Justice Willis Vandevanter to get a word from him. The interview was a real highlight for me.

For many years the name of Willis Vandevanter had been outstanding in the annals of Wyoming. He had been the cattlemen's lawyer of the so-called "Johnson County Invaders." He had been involved in the decision of the famous Indian Race Horse case. He was a close friend of Wyoming's Senator Francis E. Warren.

When I met him he had on June 2, 1937, resigned from the U.S. Supreme Court, an almost unprecedented event. He came to

Cheyenne shortly afterwards to visit his sister, Mrs. John W. Lacey, whose husband was one of Wyoming's most successful lawyers. Justice Vandevanter greeted me and put me at ease at once.

"And what are you doing in Cheyenne?" he asked.

I told him I was embarrased to say I was working on the Writers' Project of W.P.A. and intended to leave when I could find something else. I told him I was a Republican.

"Don't leave. Stay in there and pitch," he said. "Don't let a New Dealer get the job. You are doing good work. You can do good work for the State of Wyoming."

We then turned to the subject of William C. Deming. I told him I would like to get his opinion of Mr. Deming to include in the biography.

"William C. Deming," the justice said, "is a man of integrity and business acumen. He is a scholar and a man of vision. He has done much for the State of Wyoming."

Then Justice Vandevanter paused. "You can't put this in the record. Probably one of the things Will Deming would have wanted most was to be 'one of the boys'. He was never able to slap his arm over a shoulder in greeting, not even of a close friend. He has an innate timidity, a natural reserve which always seemed to hold him back."

Arthur H. Clark published the "Biography of W.C. Deming" in the usual high standards of the Clark Company. Later he published four more volumes of Mr. Deming's writings and talks. Although they appeared under my name, Arthur Clark and his staff did most of the hard work on them.

Although I never met Arthur Clark Sr. personally, I always enjoyed my work with him. I am especially grateful to the Arthur H. Clark Company for publishing my "Cheyenne and Black Hills Trail and Express Routes."

I have known Arthur Clark Jr. through the years and have always admired the excellent work of his company.

To William C. Deming I owed my journalist career. It was he who pointed the way for me to the School of Journalism at Columbia University. And he gave me a chance to become an active newspaper reporter.

THOMAS A. DEWEY

WHEN THOMAS A. DEWEY was campaigning for the Presidency of the United States I had great hopes that he would be elected, as I was very unhappy working under the New Deal. It seemed to me that Dewey had the intelligence and force to give the leadership the country needed. We were mired in the Depression.

I collected every news item as it appeared about Mr. Dewey and made a scrapbook.

When Mr. Dewey came into the West the papers gave much coverage and my scrapbook grew. The Cheyenne coverage was great.

I sent my scrapbook to Thomas A. Dewey with best wishes for his success.

Mr. Dewey wrote a personal note of thanks.

DR. JUNE E. DOWNEY

WE CLIMBED a steep flight of stairs to reach a small office on the third floor of Old Main at the University of Wyoming, the small office-classroom of Dr. June E. Downey, professor of psychology and philosophy. From that modest surrounding Dr. Downey became known, in time, internationally for her work in psychology.

Her will-temperament test, the I.Q. test and many others have been credited to her.

Men and women from her classes became outstanding psychologists and educators in various colleges and universities all over the country. The tests I remember best were those on similarity of handwriting, in which Dr. Downey showed the similarity of handwriting in families. She had other tests, too, for ingenuity, for character analyzing.

Dr. June wrote excellent poetry and authored the University of Wyoming song, *The Brown and Yellow*: "Where the western lights long shadows over boundless prairies fling,"---

I was only eight years old when I first knew Dr. Downey. Her sister, Alice, my age, and I were classmates in the fourth grade of the East Side School in Laramie, Wyoming.

Often I was invited to "sit in" for a meal with the Downey

family. The tiny mother, Mrs. Stephen W. Downey, sat at the head of the table. She was the mother of eight children: Norma, Corlett, Sheridan, Owen, Stephen, Evangeline, Alice and Dorothy. The Colonel had passed away before I knew Alice. There were two half-sisters, Beulah and Fanchion whom Alice mentioned but they were long gone from home.

The conversation at the table was always lively, chiefly about current events and politics. The Downeys talked about the same things that my father and mother and aunts discussed.

Dr. June had a glass-topped table which she was decorating with colorful cigar bands. She had worked out artistic designs with the bands. One day I accidentally sat on the edge of the table and broke it. Dr. Downey did not say a word. I imagine she was speechless.

Some readers may remember "Ham and Eggs" Downey of California, who was going to put ham and eggs on every plate during the Depression. That was Sheridan Downey, Dr. June's brother, who was a Congressman from California. That he was a Democrat deeply disturbed his mother, little Mrs. Downey, a life-long Republican.

Dr. June Downey passed away on October 12, 1932.

WESLEY DUMM

IN NOVEMBER 29, 1977 headlines in the *Pasadena Star* news said: "Leader Dies at Age 87." And on December 4, the headlines were "Wesley Dumm Left Us a Lot." "He did a lot and contributed tremendously in money and time to local projects. It might even be said that he was Pasadena's leading philanthropist of the post-World War II era. But he didn't like people to know anything about it."

"Wesley Dumm was for forty years a leader in Pasadena's civic affairs. He owned several radio and television stations. He spent his last years in La Jolla."

I stared at the headlines. 87 years! Impossible.

It seemed like only yesterday that I , fifteen years old, was a freshman at the University of Wyoming. I had been asked to take part in a chorus for a production of "Midsummer Night's Dream." The first order of business was for the director, Mabel DeKay, to arrange partners for a dance and chorus. Of the dozen or more girls in the chorus, I was the only one left without a partner. Seemingly all available men were matched up.

The next day when I appeared for practice, Mrs. DeKay introduced Wesley Dumm, a very handsome young college graduate, who had just come from the East to visit his parents in Laramie. She designated him as my partner. He was an excellent dancer with a great sense of rhythm. Our chorus was "The Firefly,"-- "Shine little glow worm, glimmer, glimmer--."

And so while the older girls eyed me with envy, I really had the handsomest dancing partner of the lot.

Wesley Dumm went on to California shortly after the play production. I never saw him again.

MARCEL DUMONT

AMONG MY MOST prized possessions is a carving of an Indian on a horse, spearing a buffalo. It is the gift of Dr. Marcel Dumont of Belgium. The carving, precise in detail, is 12 x 17½ inches sculptured from a solid piece of forest oak. On the back is burned: "Agnes Wright Spring Pioneer Historian of Wyoming and Colorado. Marcel Dumont, Antwerp."

Dr. Dumont bears the name of his late distinguished father, National Sculptor of Belgium, whose monumental work stands in "the Square" in Antwerp.

Dr. Dumont's knowledge of the history of America's Old West and South is amazing.

His only personal experience on American soil was two years in Cincinnati, Ohio when he was four and five years old. Father Dumont moved the family to Cincinnati, but Mother Dumont yearned so for Antwerp that the father moved the family back to the homeland.

At the age of eight years Marcel had his first book published. The youth dreamed of becoming a celebrated author. His second novel was titled "The Left Bank." For a time he had a weekly column on Antwerp's past in the newspaper called *Volsozanet*.

In a letter he told me "One day my father said, 'You are a stupid young man. You neglect your studies for a good profession. You write and write and spoil time. What you get out of your articles and books you can't live off that little.' That which my father said was right so I abandoned temporarily all kinds of literature and concentrated on Dentistry and succeeded and was grateful to my father."

It was in the mid-1950's when I was State Historian of Colorado that I received the first letter from Marcel Dumont. He asked if I could send him information about the Salish Indians. After some "digging", I found some data about the Salish tribe which wandered in the Coeur d'Alene area. Thus began correspondence that has spanned a quarter of a century with this talented "Westerner," author, historian, dentist, artist, farrier, superb horseman, and above all skilled sculptor.

Doctor Dumont has always been particularly interested in the Black Hills and the Sioux Indians, a field in which I have been researching, and bought many books pertaining to the Old West such as those of Mari Sandoz and Cecil Alter's "Jim Bridger". He read the books in English then translated them into German and French. Articles which he wrote about John Colter, Father De Smet and others, were published in a German magazine.

Dr. Dumont organized a so-called "Westerner" club similar to many others scattered over Europe. His Belgian group calls itself "The Westerner Rawhide Club." They have a clubhouse and grounds where they practice shooting with revolvers and try to carry on Old West traditions. The members try to portray various Western types. Marcel is the manager of the Wells-Fargo station. The Rawhide group are avid readers of *Persimmon Hill* of the National Cowboy Hall of Fame which I send them.

Marcel's interest in Buffalo Bill was kindled by the tales told to him by two elderly aunts, with whom he often played cards "in town." The aunts delighted in telling about the Wild West Show which they had visited years before when Cody brought the show to Antwerp.

When I sent the Doctor a copy of my booklet "Buffalo Bill and His Horses," he wrote a story of Cody and sent me a copy published in Deutsch.

Doctor Dumont has always striven for authenticity. When he decided to carve a buffalo on the handle of a Bowie knife which he was making, he visited the zoo in Antwerp to study a live buffalo head. He said that Antwerp's zoo had a fine collection of American buffalo, the ancestors of which had been left at the zoo by the Wild West Show.

He commented on a recent TV documentary on Denver which was shown in Belgium. He said there were scenes of Denver, the Platte River and the Rocky Mountains but "they forgot to show Buffalo Bill's grave!"

The Doctor often mentioned his faithful saddle horse, Boogie Woogie, who had a stable in a small meadow adjacent to the Doctor's house. One day Boogie Woogie wandered through the open door to the garage and fell into the grease pit where the Doctor changed the oil in his car. Dumont summoned a man with a large crane, who cut a hole in the garage roof and put down a cable and pulley. After considerable difficulty the horse was extricated and laid on his side on the lawn. In a few minutes he got up seemingly no worse for wear except for a swollen eye and a cut lip. As B.W. regained his footing two men appeared carrying rifles. They had been summoned by neighbors to put the animal out of its misery. Doctor's comment was "The men looked very gloomy when they found there was no need of rifles."

For some time Doctor Dumont planned to buy an Arabian horse for training and riding. Boogie Woogie was graying and getting slower. It was then that Dumont decided to learn horse-shoeing in order to take care of his own horses. He enrolled in a class of 92 students to take lessons from a skilled farrier. His letters told of the great physical demands the work made, but he stayed with the course. After two years of lessons Marcel Dumont was one of four who completed the course. And from then on he monthly made new aluminum shoes for Boogie Woogie and put them on.

In my youth when I was growing up on our Wyoming ranch, I used to putter around the blacksmith shop. Old Matt Bowen, the blacksmith, would let me pump the bellows and pound horseshoe nails on the anvil to make rings. Somewhere along the line I acquired a precious little volume on horseshoeing with various illustrations. One was an etching of the shoe used by Buffalo Bill in his Wild West Show. I sent the volume to the Doctor. Much to my delight he wrote back that the farrier who had been instructing him had learned his trade from the man who had written that little book.

The Doctor's intention to buy a young horse was followed by careful study of the Arabian market. "In Belgium" he wrote, "not far from my village is the only ranch raising Arabian horses. They are splendid but not great but have fine physiques. All the colts born before 1974 and 1975 are already sold."

Eventually he bought Harpa, a Polish mare with Arabian

blood, who proved to be far from a "dream mare." She was mean. She bit and kicked and "had assembled all the vices one could have." She tried to throw her rider. When she mauled Boogie Woogie the Doctor sold her.

In 1974 the Doctor bought "a nice stallion foal, four years pedigreed and papers and much money." Marcel soon realized that a colt, in order to develop muscle, must have a large space to run in, not just his tiny meadow. So he sold the colt. Next, to the Dumont meadow, came Rameses III, a beautiful Arabian, a delight to his owner. Dumont has trained him to be a fine saddle horse.

At first Rameses III and Boogie Woogie did not get along and had to be separated. Later, however, they became friends and when Boogie Woogie died in December, 1974, at the age of 46 years and thought to be the oldest horse in Belgium, Rameses grieved. From morning until night he ran around the meadow whinnying for his lost friend.

Under Dumont's training, Rameses III won in local competitions at horse shows.

In 1978 Bambino came to the Dumont meadow. He is a splendid pure Arabian. He won two prizes in the Arabian show. A horse fancier tried to buy Bambino but Dumont said he would not sell him even for a million dollars.

Since retiring from his dental profession, the Doctor has devoted much time to educating his horses and to teaching the village children the art of fine horsemanship.

Above all he spends many long hours at sculpturing. He enjoys doing western subjects with his carving knife such as cowboys and Indians, a pack outfit and the like. Son of a great man, Marcel Dumont is great in many, many ways in his own right. In September 1981 the Doctor wrote that he was now sculpturing in marble.

MRS. BONEY EARNEST - "AUNT MAT"

MRS. BONEY EARNEST was affectionately known to her friends as "Aunt Mat." She is the only woman I ever met who had been held up by highwaymen on the old Cheyenne to Deadwood Black Hills stage. A Mrs. Durbin told me how she carried $10,000 in her baby's bottle bag on the stage, to start a bank in Deadwood. But she went through in safety. "Aunt

Mat" was on the stage when it was "stopped," during the gold rush days.

Aunt Mat, the widow of an early-day trapper and trader, who had come west with the Hudson's Bay Company, was bed-ridden when my husband and I visited her at Alcova, Wyoming.

She was very alert and apparently enjoyed having us call on her.

She said she had been in Deadwood and was on the Black Hills stage coming towards Hat Creek Station when the coach was "stopped."

"They didn't get my money," she laughed. "I had it packed in my hair."

Then she told us that her old ranch home where she and Boney had lived so many years, was now under 40 feet of water.

"The building of the Pathfinder Dam did it," she said.

I asked "Aunt Mat" if she had known "Cattle Kate" and Jim Averill. She said she had.

"Yes," she said. "I knew Ella Watson. She was called Kate. Ella was just a farm girl from Kansas trying to make a living on a homestead. She was not the cattle rustler folks now say she was. She and Jim were hung over a land deal--a land quarrel. I knew Jim's first wife. She was from Wisconsin. She died in the 1880's. Jim was postmaster. Bothwell tried to run Jim off. Jim always rode a sorrel horse. When Jim proved up on some land, the real fight started."

"Aunt Mat" was a real pioneer and knew all of the old-timers in the Natrona County area.

She seemed to enjoy our visit and as we turned to leave, Aunt Mat looked up at Mr. Spring with a twinkle in her eyes and said, "You look just like Joe O'Mahoney."

Legend had it that Aunt Mat was a one-time dance hall girl in Rawlins, Wyoming. Boney Earnest was playing cards in Rawlins and cut the cards with a friend--and won Aunt Mat. That story probably is just pure folklore or wispy gossip.

But Aunt Mat well might have been a dance hall girl in Deadwood.

RALPH EDWARDS

HEN I WAS State Historian of Colorado, my telephone rang one morning and a voice said, "This is Ralph Edwards in Hollywood."

I was sure someone was joking and almost said, "Oh. Yes?" Instead, I listened.

"We are coming to Denver to take part in the Rush To the Rockies celebration, the Centennial. Could you suggest someone we could use in our 'This Is Your Life' program?"

I suggested John Evans, a banker, whose grandfather was Colorado's first governor.

"We don't want anyone who was born with a silver spoon in his mouth. We want someone earthy."

"Well," I said. "How about a woman jack packer who hauled dynamite and supplies and cables up to the mines near Ouray? She ran a string of jacks--burros."

"What is her name?"

"Olga Schaeff Little. She and her husband live at Hesperus across the mountains from Denver."

"Perfect!" Ralph Edwards said. "Send us all the information you can get on her."

The next morning I mailed all of the information I could xerox. I told Ralph Edwards that on one occasion Olga was taking her string of jacks loaded with dynamite up to the mines when her saddle horse slipped off the narrow mountain trail and rolled down the mountain about 100 yards into a big snow drift. The weather was below zero. Olga knew that she could not dig the horse out by herself, so she took hay down and packed around the animal to keep him from freezing. Then she camped on the trail. The next morning she reached the mines and brought back help to the relief of her horse.

Edwards sent a field man to Hesperus, Colorado, to meet Olga and her husband and arrange to have her come to the Denver celebration. She thought she was coming to a mining meeting. She had been accustomed to attending mining meetings in Denver through the years.

Ralph Edwards and his staff did their regular thorough work for the program. They brought to Denver old mining friends of Olga.

Olga was equal to the occasion. She received the usual scrapbook "This Is Your Life," a Ford pickup, a string of pearls and a mink coat!

My husband and I and four friends were invited to join the Edwards party at the Tiffin after the celebration. The dinner was a banquet and we enjoyed meeting and visiting with Ralph Edwards and his wife and the Littles.

Olga's husband was a gemologist and on the next trip Little made to Denver he brought me a beautiful tiger eye pin in a silver mounting which he had made. They never failed to drop by my office whenever they came to Denver.

MAMIE EISENHOWER

WHEN MAMIE EISENHOWER's mother, Mrs. E.C. Doud died in Denver, I contacted her lawyer, Golding Fairfield, whose wife was a personal friend of mine. I said that as State Historian I knew the State Historical Society would welcome any memorabilia which the family might wish to give us.

Our society director, Maurice Frink, informed me that he wished to make any contact with Mrs. Eisenhower so I withdrew from the picture.

Some time elapsed. One morning two women came through the open door to my office and walked slowly towards me. The one in the lead was smiling but did not speak.

These words flashed through my mind: "I know you. I know you. Who are you?"

And then I saw the bangs!

"You are Mrs. Eisenhower," I said as I rose and extended my right hand.

"Yes, I am. And this is my sister, Mrs. Moore. We have come to talk with you about some of Mother's things."

I told them I knew Mr. Frink, the director, would want to talk with them so I took them up to his office on the third floor of the museum.

When we stepped out of the elevator we found Sally Lewis, our assistant curator, badly shaken up from an automobile accident.

In great frustration Director Frink called for Curator Willena Cartwright to take charge of Mrs. Eisenhower and Mrs. Moore, and he departed with Sally for the doctor's office.

By that time my knees had stopped shaking, but all the way up in the elevator, my knees were knocking from the shock of meeting the First Lady.

The next morning Director Frink called to say that he and Curator Cartwright were having to go up to our Healy House in Leadville. He asked me to handle any calls from Mrs. Eisenhower. At noon that day Mrs. Moore called and asked for Curator Cartwright. She said she had an idea she would like to talk over with her.

I explained that she was out of town but I would have her get in touch immediately when she returned to Denver.

In an hour Mrs. Moore called again and asked how soon we could come to Mrs. Doud's home to get some of the things. She suggested bringing a station wagon.

Very shortly Juan Menchaca, our head museum technician, and Roy Hunt, another technician, arrived with me at the Doud home at 750 Lafayette Street in Juan's station wagon.

Detective Golden met us at the steps. A Negro man was at the door on the porch.

While Uncle Joel Carlson of Boone, Iowa, and Mamie and Mrs. Moore finished eating their lunch, we three from the museum waited in the spacious hallway where Mr. Golden had seated us. We could see a fine fireplace, Chinese rugs, paintings and many books.

Above the fireplace was a large painting of Mamie in a light blue gown.

Mrs. Eisenhower came down the stairs to meet us in a Chinese smock. She looked fresh and lovely. Mrs. Moore appeared about done in.

I mentioned that John Daehler, of the Maytah family in Boone, Iowa, had spoken to us of "Uncle Joel." John had worked on our staff. Mrs. Eisenhower said she had met "Bud" Maytag, John's uncle, in Colorado Springs.

Mamie then explained about the music album and the scrapbook.

"They are in perfect condition. Do you have something to protect them in the car?"

Juan assured her he did.

Mamie brought us a beautiful vase painted by Mrs. Doud, also a hand-painted tobacco holder and a hat pin holder. Then a jug with a crystal stopper.

She showed us John Eisenhower's Boy Scout paraphernalia and his fishing gear, plus a book on aviation. Too, there were clippings, postal cards, and photographs.

As we were about to leave, the two sisters held a hurried conversation.

"Do you want it?" Mrs. Moore asked Mamie.

"No. I have so much stuff," Mamie answered.

So Mrs. Moore went upstairs and came down with a collar box. It was beautiful. Looked like ivory. It was filled with strings of beads.

Mamie spoke of the girls of the 1890's--like Harrison Fisher's girls--with charming faces--not like the lean, athletic faces of the girls of today.

As we were leaving Mrs. Eisenhower asked, "Do you think you would like to have my maple birdseye bedroom set?"

"Indeed we would! We could use it in our museum. I'll mention it to Mrs. Cartwright."

We discussed the breaking up of homes.

"I suppose," said Mrs. Eisenhower, "some persons would put everything together in an auction but we want to give the things away to people who will appreciate them."

Both Mrs. Eisenhower and Mrs. Moore said we would probably hear from them again. The Society did, and set up a little area with the birdseye maple bedroom set, the dress worn by Mrs. Doud at Ike's inauguration, and many other things.

If you would know more about Mamie Eisenhower and President Eisenhower, read the book "Red Carpet for Mamie." It is delightful.

JOHN EVANS

JOHN EVANS, SR., chairman of the board of the First National Bank of Denver, was an outstanding financial and civic leader. He was a trustee of the State Historical Society when I was State Historian. It was the custom then for the staff to attend monthly luncheons with the board of trustees at the University Club. And there we enjoyed the privilege of knowing personally John Evans, Dr. James Grafton Rogers, Justice William S. Jackson, Caldwell Martin, Henry Swan and others.

John Evans was the grandson of Colorado's first governor and his father, William F. Evans, was one of the founders of the State Historical Society. Mr. Evans' interest in Colorado history was deep-seated. He was a large, handsome man, who stood out in any gathering.

Much has been written about the Evans family in Colorado. In this brief sketch, I expect only to mention the various personal contacts that I was privileged to have with Mr. Evans.

I was much pleased to have him ask me to write a history of the First National Bank. He was particularly concerned in proving that the bank had had a continuous existence. A banking history of Colorado had been written by a college professor which claimed otherwise. I set out to trace the actual existence of the bank through the years.

Mr. Evans arranged that I have a pass which admitted me to the bank on lower Seventeenth Street on Saturdays and Sundays and on holidays in order that I might do research in the bank's archives, kept in the lower vaults.

We soon realized what an enormous task it would be even to do the research, let alone the writing. So Mr. Evans decided to have me do only the history of the first five years (1860-1865). We set our goal for completion to coincide with the dedication of the new high rise First National Bank Building on Seventeenth Street.

I employed my sister, Alice Wallace, to research the early Denver and Central City newspapers for banking history. Together we covered five years of the *Rocky Mountain News* and Central City *Register*.

Visits with Mr. Evans in his office were always most informative as he would reminisce about various important civic affairs, not only those in which the bank was involved but also the political angles of the water board and the like.

One day as he sat looking out of his office window down on Seventeenth Street, he said, "They are urging me to move the church which was built in memory of Josephine Elbert, my father's sister. They want to move it from downtown out to the campus at Denver University. It would cost $50,000 to tear the chapel down and rebuild it."

He had not yet made up his mind what to do, but later he did make it possible to have the chapel rebuilt on the Denver University's campus.

Our brochure, "The History of the First National Bank: First Five Years" appeared in due time. We were able to prove that the bank's existence had been continuous.

I had provided the illustrations for the brochure. Just before we went to press a Denver history "buff" took a photograph to the bank which he stated was rare. He left it with the publicity department of the bank. It was added to my copy. I was at fault in not taking the photograph to the library of the State Historical Society to check it. When the brochure was printed headlines appeared in a local newspaper which said, "First National Bank Steals Colorado National Bank." There was a difference in two windows! Mr. Evans called in the copies of the brochure which had been released and had the last page reprinted with a substitute photograph for the incorrect one. It must have cost the bank $1,000 to make the correction. There was no word of criticism from Mr. Evans.

Not long afterwards Mr. Evans came to my office in the State Museum and asked me if I would write a biography of his father, William F. Evans. I was thrilled at the idea as it would have been an exciting book. The battles of William Evans and the *Denver Post* would make a book in itself.

Pressure of my office work and family obligations prevented me from doing the book.

John Evans was a man who respected the truth. He wanted our Historical Society to stand for the highest ideals and to tell things as they were.

On one occasion I debated over publishing an article in our *Colorado Magazine* which told of a political land deal in which an eminent banker was involved in the early days. I consulted Mr. Evans about publishing the article.

He was silent a few moments then said, "Adhere to the truth. If you have proof of the statements in the article, publish them. They are history."

I still have the pass to the old First National Bank of Denver.

LUTHER K. EVANS

I MET LUTHER K. EVANS when he was head of the Historical Records Survey of W.P.A. in the late 1930's. Mart Christensen, then director of the Federal Writers' Project for Wyoming, of which I was state editor, took "Doc" Rogers, assistant editor, and myself to Salt Lake City to attend a meeting called by Henry G. Alsberg, director of the Federal Writers' Project, Washington, D.C.

We reached the Hotel Utah, our headquarters, to find things in a highly confused state. The meetings were dull and uninformative. Alfred G. Powers, director for the Writers' Project in Oregon, and I left the night meeting and went to a motion picture show.

On the second morning Henry G. Alsberg was presiding. He tried to explain the changes in format for the Guides. Someone in the audience rose and said, "Mr. Alsberg, your directions from Washington are a headache."

Mr. Alsberg ran his hand through his hair and said, "Everything this morning is a headache. I am having to leave for California." And he excused himself and left.

Our writers' meeting adjourned and I decided to go to a meeting of the Historical Records Survey. Luther K. Evans was presiding. He was personable, well-groomed and an excellent speaker. I was impressed.

I decided that I would like to work under the Records Survey.

Soon after we had returned to our work in Cheyenne on the "Wyoming Guide", a young man who was head of the Wyoming Historical Records Survey came to me and said he was resigning. He felt sure I could have his position as soon as the state headquarters and Luther K. Evans approved.

I was walking on air. I was told to expect to be called into state headquarters the next day for the new appointment.

Instead, Mart Christensen, who had gotten wind of my proposed transfer, refused to release me from the Writers' Project. He claimed that I had to stay to complete the work of the "Guide", which at that stage was barely begun.

What happened next is a long story. I resigned, although I needed the money badly. Within three days Washington asked for Christensen's resignation and appointed me director of the project--the last thing I wanted then.

Luther K. Evans went on to become Librarian of Congress.

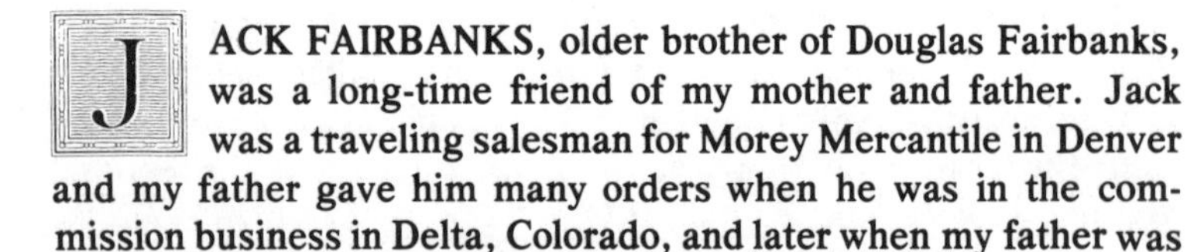

DOUGLAS FAIRBANKS

JACK FAIRBANKS, older brother of Douglas Fairbanks, was a long-time friend of my mother and father. Jack was a traveling salesman for Morey Mercantile in Denver and my father gave him many orders when he was in the commission business in Delta, Colorado, and later when my father was postmaster and had a small store in Minturn, Colorado.

One year my father worked for Morey Mercantile in Denver and it was a well-known fact that Douglas, then a youth, had the Morey Merc staff talking in their beards. Despite many warnings, Douglas persisted in climbing up and down cables in the freight elevator shaft.

Anyone who saw Douglas Fairbanks in motion pictures, doing his "stunts" would believe that Doug really did climb those cables.

When we moved to Minturn, Jack Fairbanks was always a welcome visitor in our home. I relished the oyster stew with the small oyster crackers which Mother always had for supper when Jack was there. Through the years mutual friends in Delta and California had kept Dad in touch with Jack Fairbanks, who had become Douglas' manager in Hollywood.

One day about 1914, Jack Fairbanks came to our Wyoming ranch on the Little Laramie River, to ask Dad if he could suggest a good location for a new motion picture which Douglas was scheduled to make. It was called "The Man From Painted Post."

Jack said they were to make the picture in the Rawlins area, but for some reason their plans had been blocked.

Dad suggested the Riverside Ranch near Jelm Mountain. That proved to be an ideal location and the picture was filmed.

Young Frank Clark, a neighbor of Dad's, did some roping in the picture.

MAUDE FEALY

AS I PASSED THE sales desk in our museum one morning, I heard a woman asking the way to our library. Her voice was lovely. Was she an actress or a singer, I wondered.

She was Maude Fealy, the actress, who had played many times at Elitch's Gardens and was known on the stage in England, as well as in the United States.

When the visitor asked our librarian if she had any information about Maude Fealy, the librarian brought to her a book with a photograph of Maude Fealy.

"I am Maude Fealy," she said.

She said she had made her stage debut at the age of three and that she had played with William Gillette and Henry Irving.

She was retired now and had come to Denver to live. I came to know her quite well. The Pioneer Men and Women of Colorado invited her to their meetings and I had the pleasure of riding with her to and from the meetings.

We invited her to speak at one of our monthly programs of the State Historical Society. She gave an excellent impersonation.

The next day after her performance, a man called at my State Historian's office. He said his name was H.H. Greene. His stage name was Howard Hartley. He was eager to talk about himself.

He said he had played at Elitch's in 1901 and discussed Mrs. Elitch, "The Lady of the Gardens". His last stage appearance, he said, was in 1933. Howard Hartley said that Maude Fealy's mother had a stock company at the Tabor Grand Theater in Denver. Douglas Fairbanks had played there. Hartley had played with Maude Fealy and said she had taken Ellen Terry's place on the stage. She played in *Ben Hur.* He spoke of Cecil De Mille and Theodore Roberts.

According to Hartley, Maude Fealy's second husband was Harry Court of the Court Theatre in Denver. Her first husband was a newspaperman.

Howard Hartley had played with Laurette Taylor in stock company in Seattle. He also had played in stock company in Pearl Harbor with Henry Fonda in the "Glass Menagerie;" also, with Helen Hayes and Hartley Manners.

"Maude Fealy," he said, "was William Gillette's leading woman, and she was with William Farnum in *Ben Hur.* At Elitch's in the early days we had 100 in the plays. We had wonderful costumes and sets: 50¢ downstairs; 25¢ in the balcony. Now they have four actors in a play for $3.50 or $5.00."

Howard Hartley gave me his address on First Avenue in Denver.

"Does Maude Fealy know you are here? Did you speak to her last night?" I asked.

He shook his head. "I haven't contacted her."

Shortly afterwards, before I had a chance to tell Maude Fealy about my visit with Howard Hartley, Miss Fealy was in a bad automobile accident on her way to attend a meeting of the Pioneer Men and Women. She did not live too long after that.

VARDIS FISHER

ARDIS FISHER, an established author from Idaho, was appointed state director of the W.P.A. Federal Writers' Project in the 1930's.

He came to see me in my office in Cheyenne, when I was director of the Wyoming Project.

Vardis Fisher was as disturbed as I was over the voluminous confusing instructions which were being sent to us by Washington headquarters. It appeared they were trying to make us "regional" instead of "statewide."

Fisher declared that he was not going to follow the innumerable guidelines. He said he did not have professional writers on relief and that he was going to write the "Idaho Guide" by himself.

And that is what I understood he did. The "Idaho Guide" was the first one completed and published. It was a good one. How much of it was done by W.P.A. project workers I never knew.

BENNETT FOSTER

BENNETT FOSTER, one of the outstanding writers of western fiction, lived in Santa Fe, New Mexico.

He was the brother of Trace Foster, a classmate of mine in the Universtiy of Wyoming. Their uncle, named Davis, lived in Laramie and came often to our ranch to fish on the Little Laramie River.

On one trip he brought with him his nephew, ten-year-old Bennett Foster.

Years later when I was State Historian in Denver, Bennett Foster came to my office with his young son. He declared I had saved him from drowning when he was on that fishing trip with his uncle.

My memory was hazy. The incident had not made the deep impression on me that it had on Bennett, but I appreciated his thanking me!

I was an avid fisherwoman during my growing-up years on our ranch and I had a fish pole in my hand and waded the Little Laramie at every opportunity.

I recalled vividly finding an elderly man down in the river on the riffles one day. His boots had filled with water and he could not get up. I did help save his life for which he did not even thank me.

Bennett never forgot. Ingratitude is said to be one of the worst sins.

WILL GEER

IN 1973 WHEN I was living in California, I received an invitation to go to the National Cowboy Hall of Fame and Western Heritage Center to receive a Wrangler Award. The evening after my arrival, I drifted into a cocktail hour and being tired from my trip, sat down at the nearest table.

I had wondered who the "character" was dressed in bib overalls and wearing a rather battered hat, who seemed to be the center of attention wherever he went. I was more than surprised to see him approaching my table.

He asked if he might sit down and said, "I'm the Waltons' Grandpa."

"John Boy's Grandpa!" I exclaimed. "Of course you are."

We laughed. And for the next half hour we had a delightful visit.

Will Geer told me that he had bought a used bus in Hollywood and had had it made into living quarters, with a small kitchenette. He was taking his grandson and a young friend across country in the bus. He was scheduled for a number of appearances for his impersonation of Mark Twain.

He chuckled when he told about the Hollywood police inspecting his "caravan" when they stopped on a Hollywood street to cook their lunch. He told me about his home and his vegetable garden and about the young people who came to him for training in acting.

When I mentioned that I had been in the Great Smoky Mountains of Tennessee, he quoted a number of lines from his next TV show. He had a wonderful voice and when he spoke of the beauty of the mountain country, I could see the red bud in bloom and hear the whippoorwill's call.

The next noon Will Geer was next to me in line at a buffet luncheon given at the home of one of the Hall's trustees. Each guest had been presented with an aluminum kit, such as a Boy Scout might carry into the field. We had a cup, and all the necessary equipment to take care of the luscious luncheon. Each kit had its owner's name plate. Again, "Grandpa Walton" and I had a little visit.

That night at the banquet we both received Wrangler Awards, along with others.

As the evening drew to a close, guests stopped to visit and to say their farewells. I was starting towards the door of the Hall to return to my hotel when Will Geer came up and gave me a great bear hug and a buss on the cheek. I wished him well. I saw him many times after that on TV and last of all when he appeared on Johnny Carson's Tonight Show, not too long before he passed away. That night he stressed the fact that senior citizens should keep alert and busy. He certainly practiced all that he preached.

I'm sure that Will Geer's impersonation of the Waltons' Grandpa brought to the youth of the nation a better conception of what grandparents could mean to their families. The world was richer to have had him as long as he lived.

To me the Walton's farewell to "Grandpa" was very real and very touching. Ellen Corby, "Grandma Walton", too, was a perfect acting companion for Geer.

TV Guide called Will Geer "The World's Oldest Hippie," and said "he had toured with Ethel Barrymore, drank with William Faulkner, and was interrogated by Clarence Darrow." The editor of *Cross and Crescent* of Lambda Chi Alpha called him "Mr. Americana."

VANCE GRAHAM

ROBABLY ONLY those who listened to KOA Radio in the 1920's will remember Vance Graham, a fine announcer.

I listened to him not only for entertainment and information but for learning. He was said to have the best diction of any current announcer. I studied his diction and tried to profit by it.

When I spoke at a convention of Pi Beta Phi in Chicago, I was told by one of our Grand Officers that I was the only one on the convention floor who spoke real English. Thanks to Vance Graham.

One radio program that I thoroughly enjoyed was at midnight on KOA. It was called "Midnight Chimes"--Vance Graham with Erminie Delaverne at the Wurlitzer at the Paramount Theater. They were superb.

I wrote to Vance and said I was writing fiction and wanted to do a story based on their programs. Would he please tell me where he stood in relation to the organ, etc.

Vance accommodated by drawing a sketch of the empty theater with Erminie at the organ and himself nearby. He even included a sketch of a "mop-up-ist."

I sold the story to *Love Story*.

KOA studio at that time was on East Colfax on the "fringe" of Denver.

ULYSSES SUMNER GRANT

IN LARAMIE, Wyoming, I grew up with the Grant boys--Mortimer and Ulysses Sumner Grant. Their father, M.N. Grant was a relative of President U.S. Grant. Mr. Grant was a lawyer and had mining interests which took him back and forth over my father's stageline from Laramie to the Keystone and Rambler mines in the Medicine Bow Range.

Ulysses Sumner Grant, the younger son, was my classmate. We called him "Sumner." He was handsome, quite the Beau Brummel of the University of Wyoming.

We were both in Wilbur Hitchcock's freshman civil engineering class. I was taking courses in civil engineering with the idea of becoming a topographical draughtsman, a map maker.

I was the only woman who had ever registered for classes in the engineering school. The men were fine to me but they did enjoy a joke at my expense.

On our first morning of field work with a transit and plane table on the campus in front of Old Main, the magnetic needle of one of the instruments performed like crazy. By a process of elimination Instructor Hitchcock decided that I was the culprit. When I walked near, the needle went off-center.

It suddenly dawned on me that the heavy metal staves in my corset were playing havoc with the needle.

I think it was Sumner who dubbed me "Old Ironsides."

Just before graduation I passed a U.S. Civil Service examination for topographical draughtsman, but before I received an appointment, I was appointed Assistant State Librarian in the Supreme Court Library in Cheyenne. My only commercial map work was drawing a map of the gold fields near South Pass City for the state geologist, L.W. Trumbull. I did, though, do the English hand lettering on appointments made by the governor's office.

Sumner Grant lived for years in California where he held responsible positions in engineering work in the Los Angeles area.

DR. GENE M. GRESSLEY

DR. GENE M. GRESSLEY, Assistant to the President of the University of Wyoming, and Executive Director of the Western History Research and Heritage Center at the Coe Library, University of Wyoming, Laramie, Wyoming, was at one time my Assistant State Historian of Colorado. With pride I have watched him obtain advanced degrees from the University of Indiana and University of Oregon while performing outstanding work in the field of western history and research.

As my assistant in Denver, Gene and I shared the noon hour by eating our paper bag lunches in my office. He and his wife, Joyce, then lived in Boulder and he commuted to work.

Gene was a great listener and seemed to enjoy my tales about old-timers I had interviewed.

Without realizing how young and inexperienced Gene was, I piled on the responsibility. He told me in later years that when I asked him to take charge of the Flag Day Celebration and told him to contact "the brass" at Lowry Field for a band and color guard, he was petrified. But he did a great job. He has integrity, a will to work and always had an innate sense of responsibility.

I was delighted when he joined the staff of the University of Wyoming and have been amazed at the scope of his work. Offers of big opportunities, with attractive monetary enticements have not shaken his determination to make the great success of his work in Wyoming that he has made it. Gene and Joyce, with their children, Debbie and Randy, live in a fine home in Laramie, which they built.

Through the years Dr. Gene Gressley has built up magnificent archives on the oil industry, the cattle industry, on railways, plus an unbelievable collection of music, records and films from Hollywood and New York.

These archives are irreplaceable and will provide a great wealth of information for future generations.

Dr. Gressley has written several books--all factual and reliable, including "Voltaire and the Cowboy," and "Bankers and Cattlemen."

CHARLES GUERNSEY

TOWN, A LAKE and a dam in central Wyoming bear the names of Charles Guernsey, a one-time wealthy ranch owner.

Charles Guernsey was a member of the Cheyenne Club, a much entertained young cattleman, and for a time had considerable wealth.

When the Depression of the 1930's struck, Guernsey's wealth faded. In order to recoup, Charles Guernsey wrote a book called "Wyoming Cowboy Days". He had faith in the book and was determined to have it published.

Cal Williams, a newspaperman, who was on my Federal Writers' staff, told me that he had helped Guernsey put the book into final shape.

Guernsey, who had been accustomed to living and staying at the Brown Palace in Denver and similar hostelries, was almost without funds and when he stopped in Denver on his way to Boston with his manuscript, a lawyer friend permitted him to sleep in his downtown office overnight.

Guernsey rode a bus from Denver to Boston, where he found a publisher for his book. How much money it brought him at the time is not known. But in later years it became a book of rare Americana and probably now brings $25.00 a copy.

DR. LeROY HAFEN

DR. LeROY HAFEN, Historian of the State Historical Society of Colorado for a quarter century, heads the list as a writer of Colorado history and an authority on the mountain men of the fur trade era.

Because we were working in the western history field our trails crossed many times during the years.

When the Depression of the 1930's hit and publicity was sent out to the effect that the government was going to establish projects to give work to writers and artists, Dr. LeRoy Hafen, State Historian, was appointed to head the Colorado Federal Writers' Project.

I was living in Fort Collins, Colorado, and I received a letter from Dr. Hafen appointing me as a field worker to interview pioneers of northern Colorado. I would receive so much an hour and an allowance for gasoline.

My husband and I owned a cherry orchard and had been almost demolished by the Depression and drouth. I was receiving 8¢ a dozen for eggs and 4¢ a pound for chickens! The canning factory for cherries in Fort Collins had closed.

At that time neither Dr. Hafen nor I understood the politics behind W.P.A. To be appointed to a "non-certified" position it took pull. Otherwise only those who were "certified to relief" were to be put on the projects.

I started on the field work at once. My first interview was with Mr. Pennock in Pleasant Valley. He had freighted on the old Overland Trail up to Fort Halleck. He was immensely interested in Colorado history and took me to the spot where it was said Ashley's men had cached their powder--Cache la Poudre. He told me about his wife, whose maiden name was Flowers who had an emergency operation for appendicitis. The operation was performed on the top of their grand piano. His sister administered the anaesthetic.

I went on to interview Mrs. Setzler, who owned an orchard near ours. Her uncle was the first mayor of Cheyenne. She told me he lost his life near Green River, Wyoming.

We needed money so badly and I was so happy to be doing something I enjoyed and being paid for it. I was stunned when a letter came from Dr. Hafen saying he had made a mistake in hiring me. He had been informed that he could hire only someone who was "certified" to relief!

My disappointment was so keen that never in my wildest dreams could I have imagined that about twenty years later, when Dr. Hafen retired, I would be appointed to succeed him as State Historian of the State Historical Society of Colorado!

WALTER HAGEN

ALTER HAGEN, the great golfer, came to the Denver Country Club to give a demonstration of his skill as a golfer.

His picture had been appearing in magazines and elsewhere in advertisements for Lucky Strike cigarettes.

The day he gave his demonstration at the Denver Country Club my husband and I, with a friend, were following almost on Walter Hagen's heels.

I noticed a youngster, about ten years old, with an older woman keeping up with us.

After Hagen demonstrated a golf shot and started on down the course, the youngster scooped up something from the grass.

"Grandma," he said. "Look here. Walter Hagen is smoking Camels."

GORDON LANGLEY HALL

HE FOLLOWING paragraphs cannot be classed with "the Greats" but that they are odd or sensational cannot be denied.

Gordon Langley Hall, a young Englishman, who had been a teacher in Canada, came to my office and said he wished to do research for a book on Baby Doe Tabor. I introduced him to our librarian and helped him with various suggestions.

The staff liked him and gave him assistance. He was entertained by several substantial citizens of Denver.

His Tabor book was published in due time and I had my picture taken with Gordon Hall for the *Rocky Mountain News* when the book was announced.

Hall, an orphan, had been brought up in England by a wealthy aunt. Upon her death he inherited considerable money. He purchased the Doctor Johnson home in Charlotte, North Carolina, and made it into a showplace with paintings and antiques fitting such a restoration. He sent us photographs of the home.

Hall wrote an exceptionally good book about the young sculptress who sculptured Lincoln. He sent me a copy of the book.

And then one morning headlines in the newspapers announced that Gordon Langley Hall had undergone an operation in a large eastern hospital to change his sex. He now was "Dawn." But that was not all--later the newspapers announced that Dawn was marrying her Negro gardener and that they were leaving for England! What a world we live in!

AVERILL HARRIMAN

IN THE LITTLE village of Big Piney, Wyoming, in the north central part of the state, I met an elderly man in 1940, who told me he had been a guide for the Averill Harriman Expedition to Alaska about 1899.

"My job," said the man, "was to hunt for the party. Chiefly, though, I rode herd on young Averill Harriman. He was a spunky kid."

The man showed me a little diary which he had kept on the "Expedition."

"I did kill a big Kodiak bear for the outfit," he admitted.

JOHN HAWGOOD

OHN HAWGOOD, an Englishman, came many times to the United States to do historical research. I was told at the Huntington Library that he had spent considerable time at that library and that in order to help defray expenses, he had taken care of pets for San Marino residents while they were away from home. The pets ranged from birds to horses.

John Hawgood visited the State Historical Society in Denver and I enjoyed visiting with him. He was intensely interested in Old West history. I also met him at a convention of the Western History Association.

That also is where he met Sam Arnold, owner of The Fort, a delightful restaurant near Morrison, Colorado. Sam, the son of an eastern doctor, had built a replica of Old Fort Bent and served exotic foods.

One day after the convention, my telephone rang. John Hawgood invited Mr. Spring and me to have dinner at The Fort. He said he was staying in Sam Arnold's apartment which was above the restaurant. Sam Arnold drove into Denver and took us out to The Fort.

John Hawgood graciously greeted us and took over as our host. He telephoned down to the bar for cocktails and followed with a call to the restaurant for a delicious dinner. Everything was sent up according to order.

Sam Arnold dropped in now and then to chat but was busy with the restaurant.

We had a most enjoyable evening. Not until sometime afterwards did we learn that Sam Arnold had invited John to come to The Fort for dinner. He had stayed two weeks at Sam's expense!

At any rate, John Hawgood must have been a very skilled historian. He won the $5,000 award for a book on American history.

WILLIAM RANDOLPH HEARST

ENRY (BIG HANK) was a cousin of my father, Gordon L. Wright. He was well-known for his newspaper work in the Black Hills during gold rush days. The museum at Deadwood, South Dakota, contains considerable memorabilia of Hank Wright. Big Hank's son, Little Hank Wright, ranched in the Dakotas and also was a newspaperman. He married a niece of Phoebe Apperson Hearst. Mrs. Hearst gave them an avocado farm in southern California, but before they moved down there, Hank's wife died. Hank lived on the farm and visited my sister and her husband, Donald and Alice Wallace, at their home in Los Angeles.

When I saw an item in a California newspaper to the effect that William Randolph Hearst was publishing his grandfather's diary, kept when he crossed the plains and went to California in the gold rush, I wrote Mr. Hearst and asked if I might obtain a copy. I told him that my paternal grandfather had crossed the trail in 1864 in order to join his cousin, William Wright (Dan De Quille), in Virginia City, Nevada.

Mr. Hearst sent a copy of the published diary to me.

I moved to Willits, California, in 1970. When the *Sacramento Bee* published an article about me in which I said I had done some work for Mrs. Carrie Chapman Catt for the equal rights movement, I received a letter from a woman in Chico, California, who said she was president of the Phoebe Apperson Hearst Association. She asked if I had ever known Mrs. Hearst.

I replied that I had not known Mrs. Hearst but that my father's cousin had married a niece of Mrs. Hearst.

A letter came from Chico immediately saying that Mrs. Hearst did not have a niece.

I wrote to William Randolph Hearst and he replied from his New York apartment that Mrs. Hearst certainly did have a niece. He gave me the name and address of a relative who he said would know.

I also found a newspaper clipping telling of the wedding of one Apperson niece.

So much for that!

My correspondence with Mr. Hearst was shortly before Patty Hearst's tragic episode.

DR. GRACE RAYMOND HEBARD

N OCTOBER 12,1936, all flags on the campus of the University of Wyoming, Laramie, Wyoming, flew at half-mast. Classes and scheduled social events were

cancelled or suspended. Dr. Grace Raymond Hebard was dead. She had lost a courageous three-year battle with cancer.

Said the *Wyoming State Tribune* of Cheyenne, "Deathless are the works Dr. Grace Raymond Hebard left. Recognized as the foremost historian of Wyoming and probably the Rocky Mountain region's greatest authority on Western history, her passing leaves a gap in the ranks of the American scholars which probably will take years to fill."

Grace Raymond Hebard was a graduate of the State University of Iowa, with a B.S. degree in engineering. With her mother, two brothers, Fred and Lockwood, and sister, Alice Marven Hebard, she came to Cheyenne in 1882 to work in the land division of the surveyor-general as a draughtsman. For a time she was deputy territorial engineer under Elwood Mead.

In 1891 she became librarian and instructor in political economy and science, at the University of Wyoming in Laramie.

At the same time she was appointed by Governor Amos Barber as a member of the University trustees. She served as secretary to the board of trustees until 1908.

In 1919 she gave up the librarianship in order to put her full time into teaching.

Dr. Hebard was admitted to the Wyoming Bar in 1898. In 1914 she received the right to practice before the Supreme Court of Wyoming and was a member of the National Association of Women in Law.

Although she did not practice law as a profession, she made good use of her knowledge of law. She was one of the committee of three which in 1889 petitioned the State Convention Committee asking that the right of women to vote be written into the by-laws of Wyoming. Too, she helped to write the Child Labor bill, enacted into law in 1923.

Among her best-known writings were "The First Woman Jury;" "The History and Government of Wyoming," which became a standard textbook in virtually every school in the state; "River to Ocean;" "Sacajawea," and "The Bozeman Trail."

When I was in the Preparatory School of the University of Wyoming, Dr. Hebard was the librarian. Dr. Hebard was interested in helping both the men and women students in any way she could.

In the spring of 1909 "The Powers that Be" ruled that all women participating in athletics must wear regulation uniforms. They cost $3.50! I had a perfectly good gym suit of black sateen "made by loving hands at home." I protested. Others joined me. When Dr. Hebard heard that we had rebelled, she called a small meeting in her office and pointed out several reasons why we should buy the regulation suits. She offered to hire, in the library, anyone who wanted to earn money to buy the uniform.

I accepted her offer. It took ten hours of work at 35¢ an hour to obtain the $3.50 necessary. My work, which I took very seriously, was cutting pages in the *Congressional Record*!

The serge gym suit had bloomers and the blouse was trimmed in gold braid--the brown and yellow--the University colors. The suit was well worth the money.

About mid-summer Dr. Hebard telephoned me at our ranch on the Little Laramie River. She asked me if I would like to be her assistant librarian, part-time at $25.00 a month. Work in the library would not, she said, interfere with my college work.

I would be a freshman in the fall and I needed the work. I was overjoyed. I held that position for four years until I graduated in 1913.

Dr. Hebard's library cataloguer, Miss Henry, was a recent graduate from the library school of the University of Illinois. Dr. Hebard told her to instruct me in the elements of library work. Miss Henry was thorough and trained me in all phases of the work. (There were no library schools near Laramie.)

Perhaps the most enjoyable piece of work which I did for Dr. Hebard was typing the manuscript for her book, "River to Ocean." It gave me a good background of Western history. I had taken typing in Preparatory School, so had no difficulty in that.

One day in late autumn, Dr. Hebard called me into her office and said that the Daughters of the American Revolution, of which she was state regent, were offering $50.00 for the best essay on "A Place in Wyoming Worthy of a Monument."

She said she did not think very many would enter the contest and urged me to try.

"The deadline is tomorrow night," she explained. "I think South Pass would be a good subject."

Then she loaned me some books which told about South Pass and let me take a typewriter to the dormitory laundry room.

There I read and typed most of the night. I won the $50.00.

There were other contests open to students such as the Philo-Sherman-Bennett. I entered all and supplemented my library salary with contest money.

Dr. Hebard was always helpful with advice and seemed delighted whenever I captured a prize.

The Grace Raymond Hebard that I knew was not a mannish suffragist type as often caricatured. She believed in equal rights--equal pay for equal work. She always stressed the fact that a woman should not expect special favors without working for them.

In her younger days Grace Hebard danced, skated, and played tennis and golf, winning the Wyoming woman's golf championship. (She gave me her golf clubs when I went to work in Cheyenne.)

Grace Hebard was popular at social affairs at the old Cheyenne Club, when she lived in Cheyenne in the 1880's. She was bridesmaid to Louise Swan, daughter of the "Cattle King," Alexander Swan. The wedding was the outstanding social event of the season.

About 1905, Dr. Hebard and her friend, Dr. Agnes Wergeland, built an attractive home in Laramie, near the campus, which they called "The Doctor's Inn." It was tastefully furnished with Navaho rugs, western pictures, and whatever would add to the comfort of the owners and their guests. Dr. Hebard took pride in her yard and garden.

Dr. Hebard realized the importance of collecting western history, especially that of Wyoming, from the men and women who knew the facts first-hand and had helped to make history.

She interviewed pioneer ministers, stage drivers, early teachers, cattlemen, cowboys, miners and railway workers. She was especially interested in the South Pass area where Esther Morris had served as a justice of the peace.

As a member of the Oregon Trail Commission she was active in traveling many of the pioneer routes and trails and in dedicating numerous markers at historic sites.

Dr. Hebard was a prolific letter writer in search of historical data and materials. Her files which, after her death, became the property of the University of Wyoming, contained data not elsewhere obtainable.

In 1932 when I was doing research on the Centennial Valley and other Wyoming areas, Dr. Hebard gave me a key to her office and access to her files. One afternoon she detailed for me her research for her book "Sacajawea." For more than three hours she talked about finding the Prince Paul papers in Europe, about her interviews with elderly Shoshones on the Reservation and so on. That she was sincere and dedicated to her work, no one can doubt.

She was eager to have me obtain a master's degree and was pleased when I told her I would like to do a biography of Joseph M. Carey for my thesis. Dr. Hebard presented my application to the graduate committee and obtained approval. Before I began to work for the degree, however, I was offered work which would bring in money, and I had to postpone the graduate work.

In her later years, as a professor of political economy and science, she taught classes in the University and continued with her writing. Members of her classes told me how enthusiastic she would get when she launched into a lecture about the Wagon Box Fight or discussed events that happened along the Oregon Trail.

Dr. Grace's sister, Alice Marven Hebard, was a teacher and for many years, was the principal of the Johnson School "across the tracks" in Cheyenne. Many a pair of mittens or warm overshoes were provided by "Aunt Betsy" for her little folk.

There were two sons in the Hebard family. Fred, a lawyer, who left Wyoming after a political defeat, and made his home in Chicago.

Lockwood Hebard, the younger son, made his home in Portland, Oregon. There he married Kate Pittock, daughter of the owner of the Portland *Oregonian* newspaper. When I stopped over a day in Portland, Lockwood took me through *The Oregonian* and pointed out to me a young man on the staff, who had just won the Pulitzer Prize. His name was Palmer Hoyt, the same Palmer Hoyt who became the editor of the *Denver Post.* Lockwood also took me to the Pittock home on the Heights, where he and Kate lived. After Kate's death years later, Lockwood inherited from her estate several million.

My mother and Grace and Alice Hebard were friends and neighbors for years. I lived with "Aunt Betsy" for a year, in the old Hebard home at 508 East Seventeenth Street in Cheyenne.

Few historians today realize the innumerable hours which Dr. Grace Raymond Hebard spent in pioneering in the western history field, single-handed and without guidelines.

When folks ask me why I became an historian, the answer is: Grace Raymond Hebard.

CHRIS HOLLEY

CHRIS HOLLEY was recommended to me by C.I. Leedy of Rapid City, South Dakota, as being one of the oldest Black Hillers in point of residence. Chris had a cabin near Hill City, South Dakota. He was a tall, erect, good-looking man and bore his eighty-some years well. He seemed eager to talk to me when I told him I was doing research for a history of the old Cheyenne-Deadwood stage line.

Chris claimed to have been born in Fort Laramie, where he said his father was the commandant and that he had graduated from West Point. He said that he, himself, had come into the Black Hills with the Walter P. Jenney Geological Survey in 1875.

Mr. Spring and I took Chris to lunch in a small restaurant in Hill City where he had met us, and then we drove to his cabin. The forest area nearby was badly charred from a recent forest fire.

Chris showed us a battered bugle of the 7th U.S. Cavalry and said he had served in that outfit for a time.

When I asked if he had any historical papers or a diary he said he had, and tried to open an old chest to get them. The chest was locked and although he searched for the key he was not able to find it. We told him we would come back some other day.

The next time we met Chris Holley was on the day of a big parade and rodeo in Custer City. He had driven there with a friend to meet us. He had written me that he would bring some papers with him.

The parade was a good one with covered wagons, buckboards, Indians and many men and women on horseback. Everyone was dressed in colorful western garb.

After lunch Chris took us to a memorial archway and proudly showed us a Sharps rifle which he said had belonged to him, embedded in concrete on the arch. He had presented it to the Pioneers of the Black Hills.

It was late in the afternoon when Chris took us to his friend's car to get his "papers." The car was locked and the friend was nowhere in sight. Chris tried to find him in the crowd, without luck. It was late and we had to be on our way, so we told Chris good-bye for the last time.

Mr. Leedy wrote me later that although Chris had told him

about some "papers and a diary," he had failed to bring him anything, as he had promised.

Chris died soon afterwards. I sent money to Mr. Leedy to buy flowers for Chris' funeral.

It was several years later when I was doing research in the Cheyenne newspapers that I ran across an item which stated that Chris Holley, an inmate of the penitentiary in Laramie, had escaped. He was being held for the theft of government property. According to the date on the item, it was very questionable if Chris had been with the Jenney Expedition. I was never able to find any record of his father being at Fort Laramie, or that he was a West Pointer.

I enjoyed knowing Chris and it was difficult to think he had been masquerading as an old-timey Black Hiller. Had someone had the same name? Who will ever know?

HERBERT HOOVER

WHEN KATHERINE BENNITT and I attended Columbia University in the autumn of 1916, we were invited to spend the Thanksgiving weekend with her uncle and aunt--Uncle Arthur and Aunt Jane Dwight, who lived at Greatneck, Long Island.

Arthur Dwight was an engineer with world-wide experience. Mrs. Dwight's father, Samuel Reed, had worked with Dodge in building the Union Pacific Railroad. Her sister, Annie, was the little girl in the well-known photograph which shows the two engines meeting in Utah upon the completion of the transcontinental railway in 1869.

But to get back to the Dwights. After the Thanksgiving dinner, Uncle Arthur read a letter to us from his close friend, Herbert Hoover, who then was in Belgium trying to feed the war victims.

Hoover said that he was positive the United States would soon be in the war. He urged Mr. Dwight to train a company of engineers to be ready to "go over."

Mr. Dwight organized a group of engineers and trained the men at night. I saw them drilling near the Columbia University campus.

His unit was the first to take engineers into World War I. Aunt Jane Dwight went to France as a Red Cross worker. Later, wives were not accepted for such service. I volunteered and tried to go over with the Red Cross but I could not meet the age limit of 25.

During the war one of my activities was to go with other young women from the Capitol in Cheyenne to meet the troop trains. We helped serve doughnuts and coffee. Many of the soldiers asked for our addresses and said they would write to us and begged us to write to them.

I kept up a regular correspondence with about eight of the soldiers, including a well-educated Belgian who was a prisoner in France.

One of the "train boys," Bill Barney, from the Pine Tree Division of the northwest, wrote many detailed letters, clear through the war and also while he was in the Army of Occupation in Germany. He had a fine sense of humor, and a vivid way of writing. I kept all of those letters and the little mementoes the "boys" sent me.

Long after Herbert Hoover had served as President of the United States, I saw an item in a newspaper to the effect that he was collecting letters written by the common "Doughboys" in World War I.

I wrote Mr. Hoover and told him about the letters I had. He replied personally and was delighted to know about them. He suggested that I place them with the Herbert Hoover collection at Stanford University at Palo Alto, which I did.

TOM HORN

I WAS IN THE fourth grade of the East Side School in Laramie, Wyoming, in November, 1903, on the day that Tom Horn was hung. He was convicted of the supposed shooting of 12-year-old Willie Nickel, son of Kels Nickel, an Iron Mountain sheepman. One of the boys in our grade managed to tie a paper doll on a string to an electric light cord. All eyes were on that dangling paper doll as the hands of the clock neared eleven. Tom Horn was a so-called cattle detective in the employ of "big cattlemen." That was all I knew about Tom Horn until years later.

Tom was said to have been hired by John C. Coble and Frank C. Bosler, cattle owners, supposedly to discourage settlers, especially sheepmen, from coming in on the cattle range of Wyoming.

Willie's sister married Carl Ashley, a friend of mine who lived in Encampment.

Carl had an unusually high soprano voice and he went to New York City to train for grand opera. On one occasion he stopped by Merica Hall, the dormitory where I lived on the University of Wyoming campus, and sang for us. I was thrilled. Also, I visited Carl's parents with my friends the Kyners, once in Encampment.

Tragically Carl's voice broke and his singing career was ended. He devoted his life to mining and prospecting in the Encampment area. His father-in-law had a blacksmith shop in the town and the sign "Kels Nickel" was still on the place the last time I was there, about 1940.

Everyone who knows about the Tom Horn case is familiar with the name of Detective Joe Le Fors.....According to Horn's autobiography, he was hired by several cattle companies in Colorado and Wyoming and worked for the Two Bar of the Swan Land and Livestock Company. At one time he had soldiered as a scout with Crook in Arizona, and had been with the Pinkerton Detective Agency.

Legend had it that he was supposed to place a stone under a victim's head as proof that he had performed his duty.

In the spring of 1900, John Whitaker sold his ranch to the Iron Mountain Ranch Company, owned by John C. Coble and Frank C. Bosler. Both men were college mates from Carlisle, Pennsylvania.

The partnership lasted about six years. Then Coble sold out to Bosler. Bosler increased his holdings and established headquarters at the Diamond Ranch near Rock River, Wyoming.

I never knew Tom Horn but I had dealings with many persons who had known him.

I knew John Coble's family in Cheyenne well. When their little son, John died, Mrs. Coble asked me to write his obituary.

I had long talks with Nannie Steele in Cheyenne who had nursed Tom Horn through a severe illness. She said he was a "fine gentleman." She never believed he killed Willie Nickel. It was Nannie who designed the sun bonnet used by the sculptor who designed the statue of the Pioneer Woman in Tulsa, Oklahoma.

In Cheyenne I played golf with "Bug" Ohnhaus, who had been hired by Joe Le Fors to take down Tom Horn's conversation through a closed door when Joe led him to confess that he had killed several men. "Bug" and I never discussed Tom Horn.

Frank Bosler often visited my father's ranch on the Little Laramie. When I was in school in New York City, my mother let

Mr. Bosler read one of my letters. He asked to borrow it to show to Mrs. Bosler. It was not returned. But one afternoon a month later I received a call from Mr. Bosler in New York City asking me to have dinner with them at the Waldorf-Astoria. I went down on a Fifth Avenue bus. There I met Mr. and Mrs. Bosler and an infant son.

The baby was left in the care of a nurse and my hosts and I took a taxicab up Riverside Drive to the Riverside Inn overlooking the Hudson. It was almost due west of where I lived at Whittier.

We were well-launched into our dinner when Mr. Bosler became worried about the little son. Without finishing the meal we hurried back down to the hotel. The "infant son" now owns the Diamond Ranch. In 1979 he transferred his father's papers from Carlisle, Pennsylvania, to the Western History and Research Center at the Coe Library at the University of Wyoming in Laramie.

I should have mentioned my first meeting with Mr. Bosler which was at the Diamond Ranch about 1909. My cousin, Roger Keith of Des Moines, Iowa, my Aunt Kate Wright and my older sister, Lucile and I had driven in a buckboard from our ranch to Wheatland, Wyoming, to visit relatives. It must have been eighty miles each way. On our return trip night caught us in a storm and forced us to turn into the Diamond. Mr. Bosler gave us shelter and had his cook prepare our supper.

Although I had never heard many complimentary things about Joe Le Fors as a person, I felt perhaps a good book could be written about him. Mr. Chaplin, one-time land commissioner in Cheyenne, had told me an amusing story about Joe when he was trying to browbeat a homesteader. Mr. Chaplin said it was Joe who was making a fast getaway instead of the homesteader.

I wrote to Joe who was then living in Buffalo, Wyoming, and asked if he would permit me to do his biography. He agreed, we signed a contract and I began by sending him questionnaires.

Joe settled down to the writing. He had a habit, however, of writing a chapter and then saying, "This is not just the way it happened, but I can't tell it just as it was. Too many folks are still living."

In one of his letters Joe Le Fors wrote:

"It was George Prentis told me about Horn doing the killing, before I had talked with Horn. There is many lies in the Smalley story. The woman in the country was a story writer pure and simple, and I got nothing, that I can recall, that was used as evidence. The sweater portion was of no value and was disregarded. Smalley told Stoll nothing before Horn was arrested, as he knew nothing about the case two days before.

"I was careful and written nothing but what I would be willing to swear to, to the best of my recollection. Smalley is just trying to make a hero out of himself--I could find much fault but what is the use. Stoll was a long-headed shrewd criminal lawyer of the first class."

In a letter written September 17, 1935, Le Fors wrote:

"How I wish I could see you and go over some things that I think would be a very interesting feature in our book. Something I am sure would make a great hit--you know with all that has been said and written no picture of the Hole-in-the-Wall has ever been taken. I think it would be most interesting and besides the pictures would be beautiful and it would cause only a slight delay in getting out the book if any at all. I have a car and the expense here would be hardly anything. You can come right direct to our home and have a room and board right with us as long as you want to stay. We will take my car and we will fix up lunches for the day and go to the Hole-in-the-Wall, and take pictures. My wife is very anxious anyway to see the Hole-in-the-Wall. I think a picture of those long red walls would be interesting. And also the slope of the Big Horn Mountains...Write me to Gillette and tell me what you think of it...I find my hiding place where I had to fight with the rattler has been torn down and the rock used in building up an abutment at the end of a new bridge. If you have no car when my work is over at Gillette I will come after you. I am a long way from being an invalid. And am an expert hand with an auto. J.L."

Eventually we had a book manuscript.

I submitted the manuscript to several editors in New York City but the Depression was on and no one seemed interested.

Joe began to fume. "Why hadn't he been called to Hollywood as an advisor on a movie. What was the matter?"

His letter was so sharp that I wrote and told him he could have the manuscript back if he would pay me $80.00 just for my typing work.

Joe wrote that he was coming to Cheyenne and wanted me to meet him at the Plains Hotel. His letter was more than sharp. I asked the hotel detective to stand by. The detective must have laughed when Joe appeared. He came about to my shoulder, a far from impressive figure!

Joe agreed to pay the $80.00 to a Buffalo bank when I sent the manuscript up, which I did. Joe passed away while the manuscript was still unpublished.

It was Joe who had allegedly plied Tom Horn with liquor which led him to brag about his various killings. Friends of Tom always maintained that the Willie Nickel killing was the result of a local feud and mistaken identity.

When I was working with Joe on the manuscript he suggested that I go to the Albany County Courthouse in Laramie and look through the letters between Coble and Bosler that were on file there. I received permission to consult the letters but found that the letters Joe said should be there were gone. When or by whom removed? I can't say. Undoubtedly some interesting data will be found in the Bosler papers recently turned over to the Western History Research Center at Laramie.

JOHN-O HOSKINS

JOHN-O HOSKINS and his wife, Georgana, were popular with both the college and townspeople when he was stationed as a captain with the R.O.T.C. at Colorado A&M (now Colorado State University) in Fort Collins, Colorado.

They played bridge and golf and entertained at dinners and were delightful friends.

I remember one night especially. It was after a big snow. John-O and Georgana, both tall, appeared with a small hand sled. The Chuck Warrens and other friends were with them. They came to Cherryhurst, our orchard home, three miles north of Fort Collins. I can see John-O's long form as he slid down our hill "belly-buster" style on that small hand sled.

We all took our turn at the sled and then tramped into our house for bacon and eggs with toast and coffee. What good times we did have! But what a tragic end it was for John-O!

After the Japanese invasion of the Philippines in December, 1941 and the subsequent fall of Manila, John-O was with the troops that withdrew to Bataan.

For four months those troops, outnumbered and crippled by starvation and disaster, fought a gallant holding action. They surrendered in April 1942.

John-O was in the Bataan death march. He died and was buried along the way.

ANDY HUFF

IN 1910, PI BETA PHI, national Greek-letter college organization, voted to organize, as a memorial to its founders, a school in the Appalachians. After much investigation Gatlinburg, Sevierville County, Tennessee, was selected as the community most in need of and suited to the help such a school might bring.

The Commissioner of Education in Washington had pointed out that education-wise Gatlinburg was the blackest spot on his map.

Gatlinburg then was an isolated community, inaccessible. A rude road, with several fordings of Little Pigeon River, made a trip to the Burg from Sevierville forbidding.

When Dr. May L. Keller, president of Pi Beta Phi, went to the Burg to see about establishing the school in 1912, "Uncle Steve" Whaley and Andy Huff were the ones who backed Miss Keller against the native opposition. They helped raise the necessary funds to buy 60 acres from Charley Ogle in the Burg, in the heart of the Great Smoky Mountains. Later Andy carried his children in his arms to the first classes in the school to show his confidence in Pi Beta Phi.

Andy Huff was a genuine American. He spent most of his life as a lumberman in the Smokies in East Tennessee and as owner of the Mountain View Hotel in the Burg.

I first met Andy Huff in 1922 when the five members of the National Council went to Gatlinburg to dedicate our Jennie Nichol Memorial Health Center.

The road from Sevierville to the Burg over which they had been hauling tan bark, was literally torn to pieces to make way for a new highway, so we five went from Knoxville to Elkmont on a lumber train. There Mr. Huff met us with a small touring car. Unfortunately the car broke down and we walked about three miles in to the Settlement School. We stayed in our Teachers' Cottage, but took our meals at the Mountain View Hotel. A footpath led from our cottage to the hotel which bordered our property. There Josie Trentham (who later married Squire Maples) and her mother plied us with the best biscuits and blackberry jam I ever ate.

Through the years Andy Huff was the village mainstay. He was the leader in making improvements and in helping with advice about our school.

My closest association with Andy was in 1945 when I went to the Settlement School as temporary director. The Burg had changed beyond belief.

The broad highway which stretched from Knoxville over the Great Smoky Mountains to Asheville, North Carolina, had brought millions of tourists into the Great Smoky Mountains National Park and the Burg.

One morning Andy Huff asked me if I would get our cows out of our pasture as they were disturbing his hotel guests with their early morning bawling. The Mountain View grounds adjoined our pasture. Andy suggested that we plant some grain in the pasture.

Our eighty acres stretched back up the mountain so I moved the cows up there. Then, after much persuasion, I managed to hire a man down near the gum stand to bring his tractor up to plow the pasture.

It was said that that was the first tractor work in the Burg. A number of natives sat on our rail fence like crows and watched the plowing and seeding. I was told they talked about "THAT WOMAN." But I got the job done, much to Andy's approval.

I remember one little visit I had with Andy out in front of the Mountain View while he directed Sunday traffic. He recalled the old days in the Burg with the quiet and peace of the mountains, but he was a man with a big mind and he accepted progress and took it in stride.

Andy and the other early residents of the Burg clung to their land. They would not sell to eastern investors who offered large sums. They leased their lands, improved their hotels and sent their young men and women to college.

On my last visit to the Burg one of the native young men took me in a car all over the valley and to Elkmont. He pointed out the various locations where Anthony Quinn made "Walking in the Spring Rain." Andy Huff had passed on but his fine family still carried on.

FRAZIER HUNT

RAZIER HUNT, newspaperman, radio commentator, and prolific writer spent six weeks at Windsor Castle gathering data for his biography of the Prince of Wales. To say I was surprised when he came to my office in Cheyenne, is putting it mildly.

For years I had collected data on the old Texas Trail. I had interviewed men who had brought trail herds from Texas to Montana. I had seen some of the ruts of the old trail itself in Colorado.

When I felt that I had enough data to do a good article on the Texas Trail I wrote to the editor of the *Saturday Evening Post* and asked if he would be interested in having me submit an article. I outlined the information which I had.

The editor wrote that "the *Saturday Evening Post* would not be interested."

About three weeks later Frazier Hunt introduced himself and said that the *Saturday Evening Post* had asked him to do an article on the Texas Trail.

"I understand that you have some good material and I came to ask if you would let me see it."

Then he explained that the *Saturday Evening Post* assigned such stories to their regular contributors or staff members.

"You would not have a chance to have an article you wrote accepted."

Then he went on to tell me about his own work, about his book on the Prince of Wales, and ended by saying, "If you will let me use your material, Santa Claus will remember you."

I liked Frazier Hunt and he convinced me that I would not have a chance to sell an article to the *Post*, so I agreed to box up my material, and to send the stuff to Hunt in his Bucks County, Pennsylvania home.

In due time my material was returned. No article appeared and Santa Claus forgot to stop by at Christmas time!

Later in the spring Frazier Hunt again came to my office and laid a $50.00 bill on my desk. He said that the *Saturday Evening Post* had not accepted his article because they said his leading character was not glamourous enough. He had, however, sold the article to *Country Gentleman.*

When he told me that he had used Addison Spaugh of Manville, Wyoming, as his central character, I could understand about the lack of glamour. I had talked with a number of cowboys and cattlemen who would have made exciting central figures for the article, but not Ad.

We were still in the Depression and that $50.00 bill looked about like $500 does now.

Later Frazier and his son, Robert, came by my office on their way to spend a month on the ranch in Canada owned by the Duke of Windsor.

We exchanged Christmas cards for years. The last time I saw him was when he invited my husband and me to have dinner with Mrs. Hunt and himself at the Shirley-Savoy in Denver.

I still remember some advice he gave me. He thought I was trying to do too many things in the writing line. He thought I should concentrate on one thing. "Remember," he said, "You can't bring down a grizzly with buckshot--from a shotgun."

JOHN HUNTON

JOHN HUNTON was one of Wyoming's best-known pioneers. He had wintered in 1865 at Fort Laramie with Jim Bridger. He also brought one of the first herds of cattle into Wyoming Territory. John Hunton was known as a "Man of the Country" because he took a Sioux wife, Lollee. He was criticized by some for sending her back to the Indian reservation and afterwards went back to Virginia and married a white woman whom he had known there.

I never met John Hunton but I did know Mrs. Hunton, who was a close friend of Alice Hebard in Cheyenne, with whom I lived.

Mrs. Hunton gave me information that I needed about Colonel Bullock, an early trader at Fort Laramie. She also sent me the Colonel's photograph and one of his half-breed boy, Bill, a cowboy who rode with Buffalo Bill's show.

Through the years John Hunton kept a diary, a real source of Wyoming history. L.G. (Pat) Flannery, a newspaperman of the city of Fort Laramie, published the diaries and thus made available historical facts that might otherwise have been lost to posterity.

In his diary John Hunton wrote about Lollee and told why he sent her back to her people. She was a very beautiful young woman and Hunton was in love with her. He gave her gifts and a fine ranch home, but when he discovered that she was philandering with one of his best friends, he told her to go. Although she tried to come back to him, John Hunton stood firm.

During the years he kept a large photograph of Lollee in a gold frame on his bedroom wall.

"And why not?" asked Mrs. Hunton. "If it brought some comfort to him."

WILLIAM H. JACKSON

OON AFTER Columbia University Press published my Caspar Collins book, Mr. William Gilchrist, an insurance man of Denver, brought his friend, William H. Jackson, eminent photographer, to call on me at my home in Fort Collins, Colorado. Mr. Jackson had crossed the plains in the early days and had known men who had soldiered in the 11th Ohio Volunteer Cavalry with Caspar Collins.

My friendship with Mr. Jackson lasted through the years. At that first meeting Mr. Jackson gave me a photograph of the Virginia Dale stage station on the Overland Trail, which he had photographed; also a copy of his book, "The Pioneer Photographer."

William H. Jackson had been a member of the Hayden Geological Survey, 1871-72, and had made the first official photographs of the Yellowstone National Park. His photograph of the Mount of the Holy Cross in Colorado, which he developed in the field, became nationally known. He said that in 1868 he followed the construction of the Union Pacific Railroad and took photographs of its progress.

In his later years Mr. Jackson made watercolor paintings of old sites along the Oregon Trail which were exquisite. He painted four watercolors for my "Cheyenne and Black Hills Stage" book.

Letters which Mr. Jackson wrote me during the years were often inscribed on stationery of the Explorers Club in New York City.

He wrote me about the great murals he was painting in Washington. As I recall it, he was then in his eighties.

When I was working on the "Wyoming Guide" in Cheyenne, I had a visit with Mr. Jackson in a local hospital. He was returning from having received an honor bestowed by the University of Colorado, when he had an accident in Cheyenne. He said he was looking in shop windows and did not see an outside stairwell and fell down a flight of stairs. He fractured some ribs.

He was about ready to leave the hospital when I called. He insisted on getting up to look in his suitcase to show me the medal which had been awarded to him by the University of Colorado, for meritorious art work. He was very proud of it and very humble, as usual.

The next and last time I saw Mr. Jackson was at a banquet given by the Oregon Trail Association in Jackson Hole, at the Jackson Lake Lodge.

John Charles Thompson, editor of the *Wyoming Tribune* for whom I had worked many years, picked me up in his car at Jackson and took me to the banquet.

William H. Jackson, the center of attraction at the banquet, was frail, but alert and seemed glad to see me. He was 98 years old. He reached out his hand and said, "Agnes Spring Wright."

When we had a chance for a little chat he drew me into a corner and said how disturbed he was over the fact that someone had changed a diary, giving the credit for the first climb of the Tetons to someone else. His eyes filled with tears. "That diary has been altered," he said.

He passed away on June 23, 1942, when he was 99 years old. A Denver history "buff" asked to borrow my file of personal letters from William H. Jackson, saying he wanted to photograph them. I loaned them but they were never returned.

JESSE JAMES III

JESSE JAMES III visited me in my office in the State Museum in Denver and I received several letters from him from his home in Manitou, Colorado. I never did know exactly what he wanted to do regarding his father's story.

But I was intrigued by information brought to me by a man named Fleenor. He said he had done intensive research on Jesse James I and claimed he had unquestionable proof that Jesse James was not shot as claimed. Another body had been substituted for his. Fleenor said that Jesse lived in Colorado many years after his supposed murder.

Fleenor had been a printer by trade and said he moved into different communities to gather data. As I recall it, he did welfare work of some kind in Penrose, Colorado, where he obtained data about a mysterious burial. He said Jesse's mother had also lived in Colorado.

Fleenor had amassed much information and needed someone to help him write a story. He invited Mr. Spring and me to visit his home to inspect his files.

My husband wanted no part of such business. And it ended there.

William A. Braiden, wealthy cattleman who owned the T-Bone ranch in southern Colorado, was a patron of our State Historical Society, and dropped by often to visit. He said that at one time he had a livery business in Creede, Colorado. When Bob Ford, the man who was said to have murdered Jesse James, was fatally shot, Braiden furnished "the rig" to take him to the cemetery.

GOVERNOR EDWIN JOHNSON

BIG ED," as Governor Edwin Johnson of Colorado was affectionately called, was not only big in stature, but big in his thinking. He was well-liked by members of various political faiths, as well as by members of the Democratic party.

The Johnson family lived near my apartment and one morning when I was going to work in the museum, Governor Ed fell in step with me and walked several blocks along Sherman Avenue.

Now and then the Governor stopped and said a few words to men digging trenches or to a man mowing a lawn. They all seemed to know him well.

When a young sculptress began work on a bust of "Big Ed," he asked me to assist her with information about him from our files.

When the bust was completed and placed in a niche in the Capitol, I was in the small group at the "unveiling."

Mrs. Johnson and her two daughters invited me to attend a luncheon given by a national sorority, which I enjoyed. One of the daughters was the wife of Robert L. Howsam, a big name in baseball, general manager and owner of the Cincinnati Reds (1979).

Governor Johnson was extremely fond of baseball. He had come to Colorado as a homesteader near Lay, Colorado, and served the state twice as governor and as United States Senator.

MRS. FRANK "RAINWATER" JONES

FOR A TIME when I was working in Cheyenne, Wyoming, I lived at the home of "Maw" Jones--Mrs. Frank "Rainwater" Jones. She was the mother of three beautiful daughters--Mrs. Bessie Jones Snyder and the twins, Evelyn and Emily Jones.

As a young woman, Mrs. Jones had lived in Ogallala, Nebraska, when they were bringing up great trail herds from Texas. She told me fascinating stories of those days.

But her prize story was about the "Rain Maker," who came to Cheyenne and induced her husband, Frank Jones, to let him try rain making from their two-story house.

They were living at the time in a house built by an Englishman, Richard "Dick" Frewen. The dormer windows on the second floor just suited the purpose of the Rain Maker as he could use his instruments or whatever in them.

That the stranger did make some rain fall in the drouth-ridden country could not be denied, but no one knew what his secret was.

Long after he had left the Jones' home, they opened a telescope that he had left behind hoping to discover a secret, but it held only soiled clothes.

Frank Jones had a brother-in-law, Strother, who was a wealthy businessman in New York City, with a home at Red Bank, New Jersey. His daughter, Mary, was about my age. When I was attending the Pulitzer School of Journalism, Mrs. Frank Jones wrote "Uncle Strother" about me. I was invited to spend a weekend with the family at their Central Park apartment.

A liveried doorman admitted me and ushered me to the elevator.

We had a delicious dinner in the dining room of the apartment house, at a table reserved for the Jones family. After dinner, we went to the theater to see Mary Nash in "The Man Who Came Back." It was a strenuous play in which the hero broke the dope habit.

On the way back to the apartment Uncle Strother kept bemoaning the fact that we had gone to such a play.

"And to think," he said, "we should take our Prairie Flower to see a show like that!"

Later the Joneses invited me to spend a weekend with them at their home at Red Bank, New Jersey. It would have been fun, I know, but there were so many exciting things to do at the School of Journalism with my classmates that I declined the invitation.

GENERAL CHARLES KING

SOMEONE AT Fort D.A. Russell, Cheyenne, Wyoming, pointed out an old building to me saying that Captain Charles King had written his well-known book, "Laramie as the Queen of Bedlam" there. My informant said the building was scheduled to be demolished. I took a picture of it and then decided to try to find out when and if Captain King had written there.

I wrote to General King then living in Milwaukee. I addressed my letter to "Captain Charles King, Author of Bedlam." In reply the General wrote:

"Dear Madam:

To think you would address me--who have worn five stars with 'Captain.' "

Then he relented and realized I had been using the title which he had when he wrote "Bedlam." He said that his wife had recently died and he was overly sensitive with grief. He said he had never written any fiction at Fort D.A. Russell. His only writing had been at Fort Laramie.

I wrote an apology and a letter of condolence. The General wrote a fine letter in return and enclosed a photograph of himself in uniform mounted on a beautiful horse, heading a parade in Milwaukee.

But I did not find out the real story of the old building at Fort D.A. Russell.

DR. SAMUEL HOWELL KNIGHT

I GREW UP ON a ranch on the Little Laramie River and went to school in Laramie, Wyoming, each autumn. Three of my classmates, Samuel Howell Knight, George "Bunny" Abbott and Jim Wilson, went through grade school, preparatory school and the University of Wyoming with me. They were like brothers to me.

We went to dancing school together. We read Aunt Reb'aah's "Etiquette Book" together, which we called "The Eat-A-Cat" book.

I recall that once when a strange young man named Paul Graham came on campus and asked me for a date, Howell and

George promptly came to me and said, "Paul is an ex-jockey. He drinks and smokes. We wish you would not date him." I broke the date.

Howell's father, Wilbur C. Knight, was an internationally-known geologist. He was the first head of the geology department at the University of Wyoming. Howell followed in his footsteps.

One summer Howell went to the Freeze Out Hills with Professor Bill Reed to dig dinosaur bones. He sent me the cover of a magazine on which was a young girl in a sunbonnet. He said it reminded him of me. When Howell was commandant of the cadets at the University, we led the Grand March at the annual Cadet Ball. How thrilled I was with the long-stemmed American Beauty roses that I carried with my long, white kid gloves. We women students all carried silk slipper bags for our silver slippers. There were few automobiles in those days and the walks were gravelly. Howell was in full dress uniform and wore a sword at the Ball.

My parents gave me a graduation present when I finished at the University of Wyoming--a camping trip to Snowy Range, about sixteen miles from our ranch. We had saddle horses and our big old Concord stage with its leather thorough-braces. My guests for the camping trip were: Katharine and Dorman Bennitt, Howell Knight and Elvin Sederlin, who came on a saddle horse from his ranch at Elk Mountain. My mother chaperoned us and cooked our meals on a campfire.

Our camp was on Brooklyn Lake near the foot of Snowy Range. We hiked, climbed Medicine Bow Peak (12,005 feet), sang around the campfire as a big moon rose. It was the best graduation present I could have had.

After graduating from the University of Wyoming in 1913, Howell Knight went on to Columbia University for graduate work. On his first trip back to Wyoming, he spent an evening with me in Cheyenne, driving around and telling me about Columbia.

"I can't fail," he said, "with my father's portrait hanging on the wall in the laboratory where I work."

Howell preferred the use of his first name "Samuel" to that of Howell and when he came back to Laramie to stay he was "Dr. Samuel (Sam) Knight."

For more than 50 years he headed the geological department at the University of Wyoming. He conceived and built a lodge at Snowy Range where classes in geology were held during the summer. His work with fossils and dinosaurs became internationally known. His chalk talks to his students were famous.

In December 1916, Kay Bennitt and I attended his wedding in a chapel at St. John's in New York City, where he married Edwina Hall, daughter of Professor Hall of Columbia University. "Bunny" Abbott was the best man. The Knights had a son and daughter, both geologists.

The last time I saw Dr. Sam was in 1974 when he proudly took me on a tour of inspection of the fabulous museum in the building which bears his name. The geology building was dedicated as the S.H. Knight Geology building in August, 1974. Dr. Knight passed away in February, 1975.

Mrs. Emma Howell Knight, mother of Samuel Howell, Wilburta, Everett and Oliver, became county superintendent of Albany County, Wyoming, after her husband's death. In later years she was called to the University of Wyoming as Dean of Women. Knight Hall on the campus bears her name.

Mrs. Knight was a tower of strength to me. On the evening of December 15, 1911, she came to my room in the dormitory and told me that Erle Very, the young forest ranger to whom I was engaged, was very ill. Then she went with me and was with me when he died that night. I was only seventeen and that was my first deep grief. Mrs. Knight was a silent woman but imparted strength through her dignity and understanding.

DEAN KRAKEL

DEAN KRAKEL, now executive director of the National Cowboy Hall of Fame and Western Heritage Center at Oklahoma City, Oklahoma, hob-nobs with motion picture stars and millionaires, but has never lost the self-effacing modesty which enables him to make friends with cowboys and rodeo riders, or to keep in close touch with the folks back home in Colorado.

Dean has kept himself in the background in all of his endeavors and never fails to give credit where credit is due.

With great interest and pride I have watched him advance in his career.

Everyone on our staff liked Dean when he was with the State Historical Society for a time. Then he went to the University of Wyoming Library and thence to the Air Force Academy in its embryonic stage at Lowry Field in Denver.

When the Air Force Academy was established at Colorado Springs, Dean Krakel organized the Academy's Museum and did a fine job with it. He told me afterwards that he learned much about executive work by observing the Air Force officers, who often took Dean on trips with them.

Dean Krakel's work as head of the Gilcrease Foundation's Museum of Art in Tulsa, Oklahoma, gave him the opportunity to familiarize himself with some of the rarest and finest western art. There were stormy financial days in Tulsa but Dean was courageous and stuck to his guns in relation to his job there.

He moved on to Oklahoma City to become director of the National Cowboy Hall of Fame when it was struggling for existence.

Through personal effort Dean has built up an institution of national interest and a spectacular center of western art.

Writing has always been a fine outlet for his talents. His magazine, *Persimmon Hill*, published by the National Cowboy Hall of Fame stands alone in its field. The art in it is beautiful and the history is sound.

Dean's book *Adventures in Western Art* is bringing much attention to the author, as well as to the National Cowboy Hall of Fame.

Dean's wife, Iris Kendrick Krakel, is a niece of the late Senator John B. Kendrick of Wyoming. They have a daughter and two sons.

I was honored to be one of a committee of three to nominate the first person to be placed on the rolls of the National Cowboy Hall of Fame. Chairman Robert West Howard, Forbes Parkhill and myself nominated William McLeod Raine, "king of the western writers."

In recognition of some assistance which I gave the Hall, J.D. Ackerman, of Colorado Springs, a trustee, paid the $100 fee to make me a charter member of the Hall.

In 1974 I received the trustees' wrangler award of the replica of a cowboy on his horse, for "Outstanding Contribution to the Preservation of Western Heritage" in my work as a historian.

HOMER LEA

HOMER LEA, supposedly an American hunchback, became a General in the Chinese army! His life story reads like a fairy tale. I have here only a wisp of fact but it is one that I think should be recorded.

When I was State Historian of Colorado, a Mr. Coberly of Boulder, Colorado, used to drop by to chat. I had never heard of Homer Lea until one day Mr. Coberly brought a copy of the *Saturday Evening Post* for me to read. It was the fantastic story of Homer Lea.

Mr. Coberly said he would like to have it put on record that Homer Lea was not born a hunchback. He was a normal infant, the son of one of his relatives in Boulder.

He said the little boy, Homer, was on a porch in a highchair when he began rocking it and the chair fell off the porch injuring the boy's back.

The story of the boy's career is too intricate and too long to tell here but there may be some readers who are already acquainted with the General.

E. HAMILTON LEE

CCORDING TO a story in the *Hawaiian Press*, July 28, 1931, E. Hamilton Lee held the world's records for flight hours.

When I knew him he was a pilot for United Airlines flying between Cheyenne and Chicago.

When he learned that I was interested in writing he asked me if I would help him with a travelogue. He said that he spent his vacations flying to remote parts of the world and taking photographs. He had an amazing collection of photographs taken on a recent trip into the wilds of Africa. I helped him with an article.

I became so interested in flying that I decided I would like to take a trip but I could not afford one.

When I mentioned to "Ham" Lee that I was going to a convention of Pi Beta Phi at the Edgewater Beach Hotel in Chicago, with my expenses paid by train, he suggested that I buy an air ticket one way and write up my trip and ask United Airlines for a return pass.

I wrote United Airlines and said I would write up my trip for the *Convention Daily*. Could I please have a pass for the return? I received the pass by return mail.

Ham Lee was at the controls of the United Airlines plane that I boarded on June 25, 1936. He had arranged for me to have a seat close enough to the cockpit to wear ear phones and listen to the instructions as they came in to the pilot and co-pilot. Radar was then not yet in use. What a thrill it was!

The announcement on the convention floor that I had flown in caused more than a mere ripple. I was the *only* delegate of the *500* in attendance who had come to Chicago by air!

My story of the trip made headlines in the *Convention Daily.* I recall that we made a landing at Iowa City on the way to Chicago. I do not remember an airport--just a landing field.

At the close of the convention, Adele Alfor, *Arrow* editor, was crying when she kissed me good-bye, because of the uncertainty of flying safety. I was back in Cheyenne in about five hours, safe and sound.

Adelė, who went to Wisconsin in an automobile, was in an accident from which she received a broken leg!

E. Hamilton Lee and his son both were pilots. I'm sure my first flight with him was my most exciting one.

COLONEL CHARLES LINDBERGH

NE OF MY interesting research questions came from a gentleman who was a member of the chemistry faculty at Columbia University. He was seeking information about a Dr. Land, who had pioneered as a dentist at Victor and Cripple Creek, Colorado.

We were able to locate information in our old newspaper files.

While assisting with the research, I mentioned that I had known a family named Land in Laramie, Wyoming, who was related to Colonel Charles Lindbergh.

The professor seemed interested and I told him that Mabel Land DeKay had been our drama coach at the University and that her brother, Emory Land, was an admiral in the Navy. Mrs. Gordon Land was a friend of my mother. Her husband had been state fish commissioner.

About two weeks after the professor from Columbia had done the research in our library, I received an express package from Darien, Connecticut.

In it was a copy of "The Spirit of St. Louis," with this inscription: "With appreciation to Agnes Wright Spring. Charles A. Lindbergh."

The pioneer dentist evidently was his grandfather!

J.C. LOBATO

J.C. LOBATO, Spanish-American, was a former sheriff of San Luis County, in southern Colorado. He was self-educated and a powerful force in the politics of the San Luis area.

He had swung the votes in his county to elect a governor. But when he came to Denver after the election expecting to be rewarded with a good position, he received only a custodian's job. Our museum was under his supervision.

I used to visit with him and came to admire him for his intelligence. He told me that as a young man he went to the mountains and cut and hewed the logs to build his first home. He had been an expert sheep shearer and had taken shearing crews up through Colorado and Wyoming, in season. I published a little article about him in our *Colorado Magazine*. I regarded "J.C." as a friend.

One day he came into my office with a big paper bag. In it was a fine old violin. Inside the violin was a label which read "Stradivarius" with a date and an address in Italy.

"Where did you get this?" I asked.

"From an old Spanish man in the San Luis Valley. He has had it for years. He got it from an Indian who claimed his father got it on a raid on a stagecoach years ago."

I knew that J.C. was telling the truth as he knew it. I called a music company in downtown Denver and described the violin and asked if they would like to see it.

"Oh," said the voice. "There were several models made. We wouldn't be interested."

When I told J.C. what the music man had said, he took the violin and left. I could not leave my office and follow through but I have often wondered where that Stradivarius is now.

EARNEST A. LOGAN

MY VERY SPECIAL pioneer has always been Earnest A. Logan of Cheyenne, Wyoming. When I knew him, he was a gentle little man, soft-spoken, who wore a tight-fitting black cap and was owner and manager of a rare book and curio store. In the 1880's, as a young man, he had been a cowboy on the range.

On one occasion he assisted in taking 100 horses north from Camp Carlin adjoining Fort D.A. Russell, to General Nelson A. Miles during an Indian campaign.

Mr. Logan drew a sketch for me illustrating how he had the horses tied to a huge central rope. The weather was below zero, and the physical discomforts were many.

Earnest Logan chuckled when he told about the soldiers racing their horses on the ice of the Yellowstone River.

Known on the range as "The Kid", Logan had been dumped by bronchos, had been sniped at by raiding Indians, but always managed to take care of himself.

After working for some of the largest cattle outfits in Wyoming, including John Clay's Seventy-One Quarter Circle and the Ogallala, Logan quit the range to devote his time to making spurs and silver ornaments.

Born in Dixon, Illinois, on October 2, 1857, young Logan came to Camp Carlin, a big supply depot, near Fort D.A. Russell, Wyoming, in 1868, with his family. His father, Hill Logan, was a government gunsmith. He taught Earnest the skills of a silversmith. Earnest could make spurs, decorate saddles and bridles and fashioned many other useful articles. One of his biggest patrons was George Rainsford, who owned fine horses and cattle. Logan said that Rainsford was the most profane man on the range. Rainsford, too, was an excellent architect.

About 1891, Logan opened a curio and book store in Cheyenne, which became the mecca for buyers of Western Americana and Navajo blankets. Logan was responsible for locating and preserving some of the rarest books on the Old West.

I was walking with him one day when we met an old-time cowboy friend. Logan greeted him with "Well, you old cow-thief, you."

He spent many hours with me walking over the old site of Camp Carlin pointing out just where certain buildings had stood. The area now is a part of the U.S. Air Force Base.

But the most interesting walks to me were those up and down the streets of old Cheyenne. Earnest Logan would tell me when certain houses or buildings were put up and who built them. He added many spicy and interesting comments about some of the occupants of those beautiful old homes built by wealthy cattlemen on "Millionaire Row." He knew many stories, too, about the famous old Cheyenne Club.

On August 12, 1942, he wrote a note to me in Denver which said:

"Dear Child:

I will have another birthday a week from Wednesday, October 21st, and I feel it would not be complete without you. So if you will come we will all be very much delighted to see you again.

I am also going to ask Mrs. Cornelia Mills to come and if you are bringing your car up I thought it would be nice if she could come with you.

Very Sincerely,

E.A. Logan"

I might add here that it was the daughter of Mrs. Cornelia Mills, Bertha Craig, who told me that at one time she was the governess of the children of Billie Irvine of the Ogallala, who took such a prominent part in the so-called Johnson County Invasion. When there was a rumor of the approaching "war," Mr. Irvine took his family and the governess from the ranch to Cheyenne. While they were away some of the "rustlers" went into the Irvine's ranch house and chopped their grand piano into splinters.

I attended the Logan birthday party and helped to greet the guests. One of the highlights of the evening was a chat which I had with Jim Shaw of Orin Junction, who had brought cattle up the old Texas Trail in his youth. He told me that in afteryears he entertained his grandchildren with the folk songs he had learned when they sang to the cattle coming up the Trail. Mr. Shaw was accompanied at the party by a daughter.

Mr. and Mrs. Logan had a son, William E., and two daughters, Grace Logan Schaedel, and Mabel Logan Harris. All three were highly respected Wyoming citizens.

ROBERT LORENZ

IN THE LATE 1940's when I was assisting with research at the Western History Department of the Denver Public Library, a young man came into our reading room and asked me for a little help. He was an exceptionally personable young artist who told me he aspired to paint cowboys and ranch life as Charles M. Russell had painted them. He was at work, he said, on a painting of a buckboard featured on his western Christmas card. He quickly found the information that he sought.

His name was Robert Lorenz. He was a student at Colorado

A&M (now Colorado State University) at Fort Collins. He said he was married and lived with his family in Fort Collins. He was immensely interested in the rare western material we had in our department.

When his card was printed, Bob Lorenz brought one to me. Having grown up on a Wyoming ranch and having ridden many times in a buckboard, I was thrilled with the card.

Bob's second western Christmas card was breath-taking. There were three cowboys on horseback following the Star of Bethlehem. The blue sky background and the sparkling star were gripping. Bob explained that the card was being made by a special process--new in art.

Bob brought the original of this beautiful card to me framed in a white frame. It was always my favorite of his cards.

Robert Lorenz was then so cheerful and enthusiastic that I did not realize what a struggle he was having in launching his new western cards single-handed. The cards were immediately popular with everyone who saw them.

One time, I do not recall the date, Bob wrote to me from France. He said that his work as a pilot had taken him there and that he was studying some special art. How enthusiastic he was!

I was intensely interested in his work and was pleased when in 1950, I learned he and Ed Trumble of the *Western Livestock Magazine* had joined forces. Ed was an advertising man who realized the possibilities of greeting cards and appreciated Bob's artwork. That year I went to Sacramento, California, to assist in the City Library, so lost contact with Bob except at Christmas time. For his trademark, Bob had used Lazy R L, the brand which he hoped someday to use on his dream ranch.

In 1952, Bob and Ed moved their business to Boulder, Colorado, and adopted the "Leanin' Tree" trademark. I felt sure that the cards would be selling well to judge by the comments which came to me from every part of the country when I used the western Christmas cards.

Soon after I returned to Colorado from California, Bob asked me if I had a story about a stagecoach holdup. He had painted a picture of a holdup. I had obtained a good true story in California. It was published with Bob's illustration as the cover in a livestock magazine.

According to the "Story of the Leanin' Tree," 97,000 cards were sold in 1950, on which Robert Lorenz hand-set the imprinted names of the buyers.

Bob Lorenz was visibly shaken by an injury which his small son received in a fall from a tree. A friend told me that Bob devoted himself to the boy and did everything possible to bring back his health. Each year he produced new and beautiful paintings for his cards.

It was after I had retired and was in Southern California that I learned that Robert Lorenz had moved with his family to Cheyenne, Wyoming. He had withdrawn from the Leanin' Tree and was using the Lazy R L for his "brand."

In 1965 I was deeply grieved to learn of the death of Robert Lorenz. He had great promise. Bob Lorenz had every quality that one could wish in a son. He had never obtained his dream ranch.

I had kept a collection of Bob's western Christmas cards which I gave to the library of the University of Colorado, in Boulder.

In June 1979, the Western Writers of America held its convention in Boulder. An outstanding feature of the meeting was a tour of the Leanin' Tree plant and museum with Ed Trumble still at the helm.

The "Tree" published a little 14-page brochure to acquaint the delegates with the history of the company. In those pages appears a magnificent story of American enterprise and success accomplished through genius, perseverance, foresight and work.

It is difficult even to imagine how Bob Lorenz's idea and painting of a western Christmas card "distributed from a dusty and drafty second story room across from the depot in Fort Collins, Colorado" had in less than thirty years branched into the new Leanin' Tree facility covering more than 60,000 square feet on an 8-acre site and another 30,000 square foot building.

The partnership which Bob Lorenz and Ed Trumble formed in 1950 lasted fifteen years. Ed Trumble continued on with the Leanin' Tree branching out into various fields such as the ski world. In 1979 the company published 346 artists, 367 Christmas card designs, and 400 everyday greeting cards.

The very early years featured only the designs of Robert Lorenz with cowboys and ranch motif.

"The Story of the Leanin' Tree" is a real inspiration. It should be read by every American youth. Where else than in the United States could such a story be written?

ROBERT S. McAULEY

WHEN I WAS woman's editor of the *Wyoming Stockman-Farmer*, in Cheyenne, Wyoming, I received a letter from Robert S. McAuley of Wamsutter, Wyoming. He was having trouble in getting his copies of the monthly *Wyoming Stockman-Farmer* and asked me to help. I took care of the matter and from then on I had a "fan."

From his letters I soon realized that here was a man who knew the early range country of Wyoming from first-hand experience, especially the Red Desert area.

When he mentioned that he had once been a cowboy and a cattle rustler, I began asking him questions about his early cowboy days. This was the first time I had run across a cattle rustler who would admit it on paper.

Robert S. McAuley was different. He wanted to talk about the cow-stealing business.

He mentioned that he had been an early range rider and that he even had changed brands on cattle himself.

In 1866, Bob's father and mother had been stage station keepers on the Chicago Ranch on the old Oregon Trail in western Nebraska. But because of the constant harassment by the Sioux, the family moved to embryonic Cheyenne, then dubbed "Hell-on-Wheels." Robert S. was born in Cheyenne in 1868.

Soon Father McAuley loaded his family, household goods and livestock on the Union Pacific railway cars and shipped to Green River. Thence they drove overland to Atlantic City, near South Pass.

Bob's father was a fine horseman and taught Bob to ride.

Bob wrote me: "I was extra tall and strong for my age at 10, and was a good rifle shot and a six-shooter shot."

When the roundup began in the Lander area, young Bob rode for the OX and the Square and Compass outfits.

"Since I was 17," he wrote, "the Texans hung the name of 'Old Timberline' on me. I was familiar with all the brands from Green River to the Platte."

In another letter he said: "I am anxious to meet you some time. I would like to tell you how seven of the men of our outfit were shot to death--five in the Sweetwater vicinity, and one in the Big Horn Basin--and one, Tom Collins, in Arizona while rustling on the Reservation was killed by a U.S. Deputy Marshal. I'll tell you, too, about the Texas men who left their bones broken by bullets from the Mexican Border to the Canadian line.

"Also, I want to tell you how numerous brands were 'worked' and hair brands made. I myself invented the slickest one. And only my brother John and me used it. That was after the Stock Association prohibited all branding ahead of the general roundup.

"My brother and me got Skull and Cross bones letters, postmarked 'Lander.'

"The skulls were rudely drawn on a small sheet of ruled writing paper. No words whatever, on the paper. That was when Tom Horn and Sam Berry were 'operating' for the 'Big Boys'--Haley and others.

"My brother left the country 'between two days', as it were. The last time I heard of him twenty-seven years ago he was away in the interior of British Columbia. His letter was postmarked 'Aidemere.'

"I staid while my friends were being bushwhacked--Mat Rasch--Isham Dart by Horn and Bob McCoy by Berry. I just about concluded I would rather be dead in Wyoming than to live any place else."

One day Old Timberline was in a real reminiscent mood and in his letter quoted from "Lord Chesterfield to his son." He said his father gave him a copy of the Chesterfield book when he was young.

As we continued to correspond, I kept gently urging Old Timberline to write more of his experiences. He moved from Wamsutter to Rock Springs in order to seek medical aid for a bad case of shingles.

Months slipped by with the exchange of a few cards and short notes.

In the spring of 1942, he reported that although he was past 74, "Am still a fine rifle shot and six-shooter shot. Not withstanding the hard work I done for years and the barrels of moon I have drank my nerves are just as steady as ever they were, and eyesight nearly as good, being of course, a little far-sighted. But using the Symon Peep sight enables me to shoot a high score today...I can today beat almost all of the inductees on the 200 yard offhand rifle range with either the Springfield or Giraud Army rifles.

"I have packed on my withers coal picked up along the tracks in the railroad yard. I chop up old railroad ties for kindling for two neighbors besides myself."

In May, 1942 he wrote that he had bought "500 sheets of parchment" so that he could write his manuscript on one side "a la newspaper rules."

But he said he was considering going back to Wamsutter. "Can, it would seem, write better out in the bush. I never could get used to a big town like Rock Springs."

On July 29, 1943, he wrote his prize letter, saying:

"I never was caught. Never left a clue. When in a big hurry with no time to get rid of the hide, in case a brand was on the ribs, I would cut a strip wide enough to include the brand straight across the whole hide, and pack up and cache the hide which appeared to have been cut in two."

There were many other details about the rustling work of the McAuley brothers. His tale about a skinning knife that disappeared during one of their rustling operations is weird.

When Old Timberline's letters ceased to come to me, I wrote to a county officer to inquire about Robert S. McAuley. I was informed that he had passed away. When I inquired if a manuscript had been found in his small shack, I was told that none had been found.

Some years later, I pieced together his letters into an article which Editor Pat Wagner published in the September-October issue of *True West*, in 1971, under the title "A Story that Never Got Written." I have quoted from that article here.

TIM McCOY

I FIRST MET Tim McCoy in 1919. He was the handsomest man I had met. He was a cavalry officer and his uniform added to his appearance. Governor Robert D. Carey had, on May 13, appointed Tim McCoy adjutant general of the Wyoming National Guard, with an office in the Capitol. As State Librarian of Wyoming, my office also was in the Capitol.

Tim McCoy spent considerable time in our State Library, reading and studying. He was especially interested in Indian history.

Often he stopped by my desk to chat. He told me he had been an understudy to Chauncey Olcott on Broadway, but when it seemed that success was in his grasp, his voice failed. Frustrated, he took what available money he had and bought a ticket as far west as the money would take him. In due time he reached Lander, Wyoming.

There Tim obtained work on a ranch and whenever he could, visited the Wind River Indian Reservation where he made friends with the Indians.

He concentrated on learning the sign language. After he came to the Capitol in Cheyenne, he kept a large hand mirror on his desk and practiced sign language.

Tim was an accomplished dancer and graciously taught us how to tango. Often he was the official escort for the Governor's wife, Julia Freeman Carey.

The McCoys lived in an apartment near the Capitol with their small son. Mrs. McCoy was the daughter of the eminent New York actor, Henry Miller.

In February, 1921, I resigned as State Librarian to be married to Archer T. Spring, a geologist. Tim left the Capitol four months later on June 14 and went to California.

I wrote an article about him, using a photograph of him talking sign language to an Indian chief and sold the article to *Sunset Magazine* in San Francisco.

Tim wrote me to thank me for the article and said that Carl Laemmle of Famous Players had read the article and had sent for him. He asked him to take charge of the Indians for the Prologue of the big motion picture, "The Covered Wagon." Tim took the Indians to England for the Prologue.

I had discussed with Tim McCoy the book which I hoped to write about Caspar Collins, the hero of the Platte Bridge Fight, who was killed by Indians in 1866. Tim suggested that I ask General Hugh L. Scott to write an Introduction to my book. General Scott, he said, was a five star general, a recognized authority on Indians, and was a personal friend of McCoy.

Because of Tim's friendship, General Scott wrote the Introduction. On March 2, 1927, General Scott wrote:

Foreword

In writing a brief preface to this work I must rejoice in the printing and making available to the public another link in history of the Western Plains, over which I have ridden more than 10,000 miles on horseback and which I love with the love of my youth spent among the Indians, the antelope and the buffalo, and whose history is dear to my heart.

My wife's father, General Merrill, was stationed at Fort Laramie in 1855 and I have heard him tell of meeting Sir George Gore there and that grand old man of the mountains, Major James Bridger, the peer of all the mountain men and guides of the West. I have been thrown intimately with General Grenville Dodge, chief engineer of Sherman's march to the sea, as well as of the Union Pacific Railway, a great friend and admirer of Bridger's, concerning whom any little bit of additional information is most acceptable.

I have heard much of Caspar Collins during the past forty years, but never so much as is revealed in the work concerning Collins, the boy and the man, of Pilgrim ancestry. He was one of the hardy American stock from Kentucky and Ohio that played a great part in the settlement of the West.

No doubt the scenes portrayed in "The Covered Wagon" that purport to show the localities mentioned in this book and the life of those times will serve to give added interest to the work.

I have passed lately several times through the city of Casper, where no doubt as elsewhere on the Plains there are many people to whom the name of Caspar carries no historical association and who know nothing of the suffering and sacrifices of the American Army. The benefits of these heroic actions are reaped by the latter generation to whom I recommend a perusal of this work with gratitude.

Hugh L. Scott

The book was published by Columbia University Press in 1927. Forty-two years later in 1969, the University of Nebraska Press, Lincoln, Nebraska, reprinted the book as one of their Bison paperbacks.

About 1928 Tim McCoy wrote me saying that he was organizing a Wild West Show to take to the second Centennial Exposition in Philadelphia, that summer.

"Do you think," he asked, "that the *Sunset Magazine* would use a second article about me?"

I told him I was sure they would and that I would be glad to write it. The editor of the *Sunset Magazine* said they certainly would like a second article about Tim McCoy and they published it.

Through the years Tim McCoy starred in many motion pictures and rode the Wild West Show circuit until the time of his death at 88 years, in 1978.

When I knew him in Cheyenne, he had written and published a little booklet of western poems. I especially like the one called "Little Dogie." Tim had a splendid sense of rhythm and could express pathos as well as joy. The copy of the poems which he gave me was placed long ago with my files in the Western Research Center at the University of Wyoming.

About 1977 I wrote Tim at his ranch near Nogales, Arizona, and asked if by any chance I could get another copy of his poems, especially of "Little Dogie."

Tim wrote back that he did not have a copy but said he could remember the poem. He sent me a hand-written copy of "Little Dogie."

Tim had two fine sons who served with the armed forces, as he did, in World War II.

His second wife, whom he married after World War II, was Inga Arvad, a Danish newspaper columnist, who scooped her Berlin colleagues by breaking the story that Herman Goering, head of the German Air Force, would marry the German actress, Emmy Sudenberg. Invited to the wedding, Inga met the high ranking Nazis who were ruling Germany at the time.

During World War II Inga came to the United States to write for the *Washington Times-Herald.* She quit journalism to marry Tim McCoy.

She died at their ranch home at Nogales, Arizona, in December 1973. (See article on Tim McCoy in *Frontier Times* April-May 1972.)

MRS. GUS CRAVEN - DENVER McGAA'S DAUGHTER

NOWLEDGE OF OUR family history was vague when I stopped in Chicago on my way to Columbia University, to see "Uncle Folsom" Dorsett.

When he said to me, "I helped found Denver," I listened but I did not know what he was talking about. He told me that he and his two Dorsett brothers, William and Rudolph, had been in Denver in 1859 and that he had been a member of the Denver

Town Company. He said he had traded his lot in Denver for a horse and saddle and had returned to Iowa to go into the Civil War.

When I later became State Historian of Colorado and examined the old records, I found Uncle Folsom Dorsett indeed was one of the original members of the Denver Town Company! He had gone to Denver with the Larimers. I also learned that Denver McGaa was the son of "Jack Jones" McGaa who had been living on the site of Auraria when the gold rush began.

All of which is by way of explanation to account for my surprise when a little woman named Mrs. Gus Craven and her son Ted came into my office.

"Could I please see my father's papers?" she asked. "His name was McGaa. His father was William McGaa. He owned the land where Denver now stands."

"Denver McGaa?" I asked.

She nodded.

Our librarian found the precious papers pertaining to land which Denver McGaa had given to Denver. The papers seemed definite and there was nothing we could do to help the visitor further.

We had a very good visit.

Suddenly the thought reached me when Mrs. Craven rose to go that the newspaper would love a story about her. She was the daughter of an Englishman who had married a Sioux woman. It was closing time at the museum and the five o'clock traffic rush was on outside.

I called Jack Foster, editor of the *Rocky Mountain News*, and told him about Mrs. Craven and her son, Ted, who had come the long way from their ranch in Dakota.

Jack said, "Keep her there. We'll have a reporter there in five minutes."

Then I heard a siren screeching in and out of the traffic on Fourteenth Avenue. A police car pulled up to the museum and a reporter and a photographer arrived at my office.

The next morning the *Rocky Mountain News* carried a half-page picture of the daughter of Denver McGaa and her son Ted.

The thought of the dear little woman riding all night on a bus worried me. I had grown fond of her during our visit. I pinned a pink carnation on her coat lapel and kissed her good-bye. I woke several times in the night thinking of that long bus ride!

The next day when one of our staff members saw Mrs. Craven's picture in the *News*, he said, "Mrs. Gus Craven! Her husband was a cattleman who bred purebred Herefords. Mrs. Craven exhibited stock at the National Western a number of times and took ribbons! She is well-to-do!"

I hoped she had a safe journey home.

GOVERNOR STEVE McNICHOLS

GOVERNOR STEVE McNICHOLS was interested in preserving the history of Colorado, and personally participated in various historical meetings. He was at the dedication of our museum at old Fort Vasquez near Platteville and spoke. He also spoke at the dedication of a plaque in Dead Man's Canyon near Colorado Springs. His young son also was in our group and I enjoyed talking to him. Although he was only about ten years old he was editing a little neighborhood news sheet. I understood that when he had finished school he was with a television station in Greeley.

When the City of Denver held a ceremony at the opening of its new tourist center, near the old city library building, I attended. Even though I was State Historian, there was no reason that I should receive any special attention as this was a City of Denver matter.

I was standing with a group near the tourist center when the ceremony was about to begin. I saw Governor Steve McNichols leave the speaker's stand. He came down and escorted me to a seat on the platform.

Steve's father was prominent in Denver politics and his brother, William (Bill), was elected for the third term as mayor of Denver in 1979.

ANDREW MANSEAU

ANDREW MANSEAU answered my knock at the door of his cabin home at Burris, Wyoming, near Dubois.

When I explained that Reverend John Roberts of Wind River had suggested I talk with him, he stepped outside of the cabin, picked up two stools and carried them into the yard. He invited me to sit down.

"My wife," he said in a low voice, "is cleaning house and doesn't want anyone in there. She's 84. I'm 82, myself." He winked.

Then he said he had married his uncle's widow.

I asked him if he ever had heard of Sacajawea, Basil's mother, on the reservation.

"I knew an old Indian woman," he said, "a Shoshone, who used to buy meat from me. They said she had been on an expedition to the ocean. She talked about the big fish on the beach. She told the storekeeper that the fish would stretch from the store way out--a long way."

"Did you ever talk with her about her early life?" I asked.

"No. Reverend Roberts buried the old woman who used to buy meat from me. He ought to know all about her."

Then Manseau changed the subject. "I've met a lot of old-time folks," he said. "I knew Butch Cassidy. He used to buy hay from me--blue point. Lots of it. In winter he'd feed horses on my ranch just down the river from me. Sometimes he slept with me when he was running horses up the Wind River. He and his gang would steal horses in Dakota then run them into Wyoming and take them through Jackson Hole to Utah. They'd sell the horses there, then steal horses there and drive them into Wyoming and take them to the Dakotas to sell."

Manseau told me about some of the troubles he had had and would have talked longer but the sun was getting low and I had to be on my way. Just before I left him, a youngster came around a big rock carrying a bow and arrow. He had a little dog with him.

"That's the grandson of Teton Jackson," Andrew nodded.

"Teton Jackson? The outlaw?"

"Yep. Teton settled down and moved to Lander," Manseau assured me.

Then he told me more about Teton Jackson, but that's another story.

ELWOOD MEAD

MY FRIENDS IN Fort Collins, Colorado, knew I was interested in writing and often gave me tips for stories. One night my dinner partner, Charles Lowell, owner of a hardware store, said, "I think you can get a good story at the college. They are building a model for a big dam to be built on the Colorado River. We are selling them tin and other necessary materials for the model. They refer to it as Hoover Dam for President Hoover."

I went to the Irrigation Engineering Department at Colorado Agricultural and Mechanical College (now Colorado State University).

When I asked the man in charge if I could do a story about the model, he said that he was a United States Government employee but had no authority to release any publicity.

I went home and tried to think who might help me. I knew that Elwood Mead, then U.S. Commissioner of Reclamation, had graduated from "Aggies" and that he also had been Territorial Engineer of Wyoming. Too, I recalled that Dr. Grace R. Hebard had been his deputy when he was territorial engineer. I had been her assistant. I wrote to Mr. Mead and asked for permission to do a story on the model dam.

He gave me his permission and authorized the men in charge of the project to run water through the model for a photograph.

The men at the college gave perfect cooperation. The photographer got set and the machinery to run the water was put into motion.

Just as the camera snapped, the man who was operating the model stepped aside. When the photograph was developed the man was headless. I was dismayed, as it was quite a deal to put the model into action. I hesitated to ask to have the water run again.

"Don't worry," said the man in charge. "We'll put another head on the photograph."

They did.

I sold the article--the first publicity on the Hoover Dam Model--to Peter Edson of the NEA, a newspaper syndicate, for $100.00, thanks to Elwood Mead and the tip from Charles Lowell.

"DOC" MIDDLETON

DOC MIDDLETON was known as an outlaw who stole horses in Nebraska and possibly in eastern Wyoming.

When I was director of the Wyoming Writers' Project, one of my field workers, Dr. O. Kongslie, a chiropractor of Newcastle, Wyoming, wrote me that he could arrange an interview for me with a Mr. Richardson, a brother-in-law of "Doc" Middleton. Richardson was writing a story about "Doc."

On my next field trip to Newcastle I went to the Kongslie home to talk with Richardson.

Doctor Kongslie had said with a smile that Richardson was apt to get overly friendly, then he introduced us.

We sat down on a couch in Kongslie's office.

We were well launched into reading the manuscript about "Doc" Middleton when suddenly the elderly visitor hitched over next to me. I moved away and in another second we both were dumped in a heap on the floor.

Dr. Kongslie's "couch" was a chiropractor's table for examining patients and was very mobile!

I did, though, manage to borrow the manuscript on "Doc" Middleton from Richardson. It was well worth reading.

Mr. Richardson, who lived on a ranch near Newcastle, spent his winters in Phoenix, Arizona.

GENERAL BERNARD MONTGOMERY

I WAS DEEPLY concerned during World War II over Rommel's drive against the British in Africa. I was listening to a radio announcer reporting on the British being driven towards Egypt by Rommel's troops in the Battle of El Alamein. The report was so vivid that I could not see how the British could escape that advancing army. Then suddenly the tide turned at Alamein. Field Marshal Bernard Montgomery saved the day. Rommel's men were cut off from their supply train. The defeat was tremendous.

I had never been a collector of autographs but through the years I kept clippings about Montgomery and decided I would like to have his autograph.

I contacted him through his bank in London and told him how I had listened on the radio to that fateful day in 1942 in the war.

General Montgomery wrote a nice note in reply and signed it: "Montgomery Alamein."

I kept this letter in my locked steel file with my most precious antiques and jewelry, bonds and the like. Although my apartment was in a locked apartment house with a security guard living inside, someone broke into my file and took all of my valuables, including the General's letter in August, 1977, while I was on vacation in Wyoming. No trace of the stolen things has been found.

MRS. ANNIE D. MORRIS

MRS. ANNIE D. MORRIS, a social leader in Denver for many years, was named "Queen of the Islands," by the Royal Hawaiian Hotel in Honolulu, because she had spent twenty-five winters in Hawaii.

Her daughters, Mary Brown Lowell and Sally Brown Whitaker, and their families lived in Fort Collins and were close friends of my husband and me.

We were invited to Mrs. Morris' home in Denver and also to spend a weekend at the ranch she owned on the Blue River near Dillon, Colorado.

Fred Brown, her son, was a broker with Boettcher-Newton in Denver. We often saw Fred and his first wife, Lucy Ravenscroft Brown.

One evening when Mr. Spring and I were living in Denver, where he was employed with Remington Arms, Mary Lowell called us and asked if I could come to her mother's home and bring my typewriter.

She said that the doctor had told the family that Mrs. Morris could not live through the night, and they knew that the Denver newspapers would want data about her mother. They needed my help.

I arrived at the home of Mrs. Morris on Marion Street about six o'clock in the evening. Members of the family were trying to record dates and information.

I realized then, as I had done before on other occasions, that families should be prepared for such a situation. Memories could not be trusted for accuracy.

Mrs. Morris passed away about half-past nine that evening. I typed an obituary, with the help of the family, and took it to the *Post* and *News* that night.

The funeral was held in her home among the beautiful things Mrs. Morris had collected in her travels. I had been calm up until the closing song. And when the strains of the closing song, "Aloha," reached me, I was torn apart.

MRS. ESTHER MORRIS

I DID NOT KNOW Mrs. Esther Morris whose statue stands in front of the Capitol in Cheyenne, Wyoming, but I did know her son, Robert, and her nephew, Robert Dubois.

Robert Morris had served as secretary of the Wyoming Historical Society and later lived in Green River, Wyoming, where a small marker was placed in his honor in front of the library.

Mrs. Esther Morris was appointed the first woman justice of the peace in Wyoming. Her home then was in South Pass City. Later she lived in Laramie with the son of her first marriage, Edward A. Slack, a newspaperman.

Mary G. Bellamy, who knew Mrs. Morris well, told me of her kindness to needy persons. Mrs. Morris would take her baby buggy to the Union Pacific tracks in Laramie and pick up coal to take to the poor.

She was a strong advocate of women's rights.

DR. NOLIE MUMEY

WHEN ARCHER, my husband, was called to the Remington Arms Plant in Denver on the day Pearl Harbor was attacked, I resigned my directorship with the "Wyoming Guide" and followed him to Denver. We were lucky to find an apartment at 1314 Elizabeth Street. It was a one flight walk-up apartment. My door bell rang. I opened the door to see a gentleman in a palm beach suit with a red carnation in his buttonhole. He carried a package.

"I am Nolie Mumey," he said. "Welcome to Denver. I've wanted to meet you. I've read some of your writings."

Then he presented to me a copy of his rare book, "Jim Baker." At that time it was valued at about $50.00.

I had thought that the author of "Jim Baker" was a college professor. I soon learned that Dr. Mumey was a skilled surgeon and practicing physician.

On that day in the spring of 1942 there began a friendship which has lasted almost forty years! We both have been intensely interested in western history and writing. I welcomed the chance to help now and then with some research.

Dr. Mumey has given me many fine volumes of his writings. He has been a man of amazing vitality, accomplishing many things in addition to carrying on his medical practice. He was a tower of strength during my husband's illnesses.

The Doctor brought a marvelous woven rain cape to me from Argentina; an onyx pin from Mexico, and innumerable other things. He has always looked for new horizons and shipped out on a freighter from Ecuador to visit the exotic Easter Island.

He led many a bus tour to historic sites in Colorado which I thoroughly enjoyed, including a trip to Sand Creek Battle site, and a visit to Cripple Creek and Victor.

Dr. Mumey loves the great outdoors and enjoys fishing, from Canada to Mexico. Every Christmas he sends a book of his poems based on a thought for each day of the year.

In his later years he has taken up silversmithing and gem cutting. A silver bracelet set with a turquoise which he sent to welcome me back to Colorado, was beautiful.

At 88 in 1979, he attended school one week a year to keep his medical license active and still carries on his medical practice.

He amazed me one day when he turned to my husband as we were visiting in his office and said: "I think as much of this woman as you do."

The Doctor has always been a great collector of artifacts, Kachina dolls, rare books, and dozens of historical objects. He was particularly interested in the restoration of Fairplay with its museum. He had made a wax figure of a dance hall girl and was taking it up through South Park to Fairplay. He had the figure partially covered in the back seat of his car. When he stopped at a filling station the attendant thought he had a dead woman in his car and when he pulled away, called the sheriff. The Doctor was stopped en route!

The poems reveal the depth of this versatile man. They are filled with philosophy, comfort and wise advice.

They really broke the mold when they made Dr. Nolie Mumey.

JAMES MURRAY

IMMY MURRAY was a pilot with the RAF in World War I. I knew him when he was flying the mail for United Air from Cheyenne to Salt Lake. He flew an open cockpit plane. Jimmy Murray and other pilots boarded at the Brownee Boarding House in Cheyenne where some of us from the Capitol boarded.

Jimmy fell in love with Evelyn Jensen, my assistant librarian. Now and then he would circle the Capitol dome and wave to us from the open cockpit.

One Saturday Jimmy and his friend, Vincent Carter, assistant attorney general, invited Evelyn and me to go to a football game with them in Fort Collins, Colorado. On our way back to Cheyenne Jimmy said that he was flying the mail the next morning to Salt Lake City. There was no radar in those days, and the pilots were instructed to fly over the telegraph lines along the Union Pacific Railway.

"But," said Jimmy. "I'm going to cut across on the return and come back over Snowy Range. I can cut a lot of distance."

When his return plane did not reach Cheyenne on schedule we knew he must have had an accident. We did not dare to tell he had planned to cut across country.

Planes went out in search for him. After about ten hours we received word that Jimmy's plane had crashed but he was not seriously injured. He had walked into Arlington, where rescuers met him.

He told us later that when he neared Snowy Range he could not elevate his plane. He saw he would hit the range, so followed the instructions he had learned in the RAF. He nosed the plane down and lit in the top of a pine tree. He received slight cuts from his goggles. Oddly enough his father died at this time sitting in his rocking chair back east.

As I recall it, Jimmy took some of his salary in airline stock. He later became vice president of Boeing with headquarters in Washington, D.C.

Soon after Mr. Spring and I were married, Jimmy and Evelyn were married. For our wedding present he gave us a beautiful Japanese tea set--cherry blossoms on pink.

JOHN MYERS MYERS

I HAD RETIRED as State Historian and was living in The Camelia House on Grant Street in Denver when John Myers Myers, a Mesa, Arizona, writer called on me. He said he was interviewing pioneers to gather data for a book about the last of the old westerners. He asked if I would tell him something about my early years in Wyoming.

I knew he had a very small tape recorder in one hand but had no idea how much of our conversation he really recorded. He was pleasant and really knew the Old West. I enjoyed chatting with him about our old Wyoming ranch life.

Several months after his visit, he sent me a copy of his book called the "Last of the Westerners." He had devoted a chapter called "Stagestop," to the early days when our ranch home was the stagestop on my father's stage line. Whoever had transcribed Myers' tape had made a number of errors.

Not long after the book appeared, Jim Bishop of ABC in New York City contacted me asking if I would give my permission to use the chapter in a TV documentary called "The Last of the Westerners."

I replied that I would not give consent until I had corrected the errors.

I was then living in Longmont, Colorado, with my sister, Alice Wallace.

Soon I received a call from Jim Bishop saying he would like to talk to me. Within a few hours he arrived at our apartment with two cameramen, a scriptwriter, a director--five in all.

My sister served coffee and cinnamon rolls while the men set up their cameras in our kitchen. Jim Bishop said they were planning to make the film in the Leadville area.

Suddenly the skies opened and great snowflakes came down, burying everything in a white blanket. Jim Bishop looked stunned.

"We won't make any TV documentary in such weather. What must it be like in Leadville? Can you come to Arizona? We'll take care of all expenses."

And thanks to the snow, I went to Scottsdale to Valley Ho and worked several days on the ABC documentary at the Pioneer Village about eighteen miles from Scottsdale.

The center of our activity was a little old cabin similar to one my father had used. It was "under the lights" about six hours a day.

We would leave Valley Ho after breakfast and go by automobile to Pioneer Village. At noon we had lunch in a mobile home or trailer and about 6:00 we would get back to Valley Ho.

After showering and dressing for the evening we went out on

the town--to a special Italian or a French restaurant.

According to the scriptwriter the close of my part was to be quite nostalgic. I was to lean against a post on the cabin porch just as the sun was dropping behind a hill. I was to say, "The Old West faded for me--."

Everything was ready. The sun was nearing the horizon. The director shouted, "Just three minutes." And then something broke. The machine did not record and the sun was out of sight.

Pandemonium broke loose. Some of the crew acted like prima donnas.

Jim Bishop was calm, but said I would have to stay over another day. I did. But the afternoon was overcast. There was no sunset and the documentary was completed by lights.

John Myers Myers and his wife were present during some of the filming and when the work was completed they took me to their home near Mesa for lunch. At my request they left me at a motel near the Superstition Mountains.

When the documentary, which was sponsored by 3M was aired, my sister and I were entertained at dinner at the Laffite in Denver by Mr. Leasure of KBTV-Channel 9--ABC. After dinner we watched "The Last of the Westerners" in color in Mr. Leasure's office.

WILEY OAKLEY

ILEY OAKLEY was known as "The Man of the Mountains," when I used to visit our Pi Beta Phi Settlement School in Gatlinburg, Tennessee. Wiley's children had attended our school and he regarded everyone connected with it as his friends.

One Sunday when I was acting director of the school, his daughter Sue invited me to take a walk with Wiley and herself. Both of them were skilled woodsmen. And what a walk that was!

Wiley knew every bird call and could detect the cry of a wee bee bird or could hear an airplane long before I could. Both of them pointed out the most exotic flowers and shrubs, identified the birds and trees and made the whole woods come to life for me. Wiley had been a professional guide in the Great Smoky Mountains for many years.

Sue Wiley had collected the folk songs of the mountains for years and told me that she had a notebook full of the songs and expressions of the mountain folk. One day a man named John Jacob Niles visited the Burg and was fascinated with her notebook of folk songs. He borrowed the book but it was never returned. I had been going to the Burg since 1922 and always loved to hear the folk songs.

Wiley told me a wild tale about being kidnapped by two women in a big limousine. He said they took him to New York to a radio station. They wanted him to talk over the radio just the way he did when he was guiding in the mountains.

His description of the radio broadcast was priceless. He knew what his captors had in mind but he played innocent. Finally, though, after he did talk on the radio, he received an offer of a $10,000 contract from a soap company, if he would do a regular program.

Wiley said, "I didn't want any of it. All I wanted was to get back home to the Burg." He knew his wife would "be plumb scairt over me being gone."

Wiley autographed the book he had written for me. My "for free" tour was one of the most interesting tours I ever took.

DONALD R. ORNDUFF

IN NOVEMBER 10, 1980, Donald R. Ornduff, a long-time friend, was installed in Heritage Hall of the American Hereford Association of Kansas City, Missouri, during the American Royal. Retired Editor Donald R. Ornduff's name had appeared on the masthead of the *American Hereford Journal* for more than 50 years.

It was back in 1936 when I was on the staff of the *Wyoming Stockman-Farmer* in Cheyenne, Wyoming that Editor Ornduff asked me if I would do an article for his *Journal* on Hon. Joseph M. Carey and his sons, Robert D. and Charles, who had won international recognition for their prize-winning Hereford cattle raised at The Meadows, the CY Ranch near Casper, Wyoming, and at Careyhurst near Douglas.

I was a great admirer of the Careys as I had served as State Librarian-State Historian under Governors Joseph M. and Robert D. Both had been United States Senators, as well as governors of Wyoming. I knew Charlie and his wife, Nellie, who lived in Cheyenne and ran The Meadows.

My Carey article was published in the *American Hereford Journal.*

Next, Editor Ornduff asked me to do an article for the *Journal* about the exotic old Cheyenne Club, established in the early 1880's by a small group of wealthy young Eastern college men who were joined by titled Britishers and a talented Frenchman. All were adventuresome cattlemen, excited over the western range country. They ran their Cheyenne Club with all of the comforts and niceties of an exclusive club in New York or London.

I had been collecting historical data on the Club and enjoyed doing the assignment.

As I recall it, Editor Ornduff published the article in the annual edition of the *Journal* and then had 100 copies run off and bound in a neat little brochure. He sent 25 copies to me. I gave twenty-three copies as Christmas gifts to relatives and friends.

As the years slipped by and the horizon was being dotted with collectors of Western Americana, my "Cheyenne Club" item was sought by collectors. I understood that about 1978 one copy sold in Texas for $80.00. Where are my gift ones now?

Editor Ornduff suggested that I do an article on "Culture in the Cow Country." He said he felt there was a good story there.

I wrote him that it was the kind of story that depended largely on serendipity, but that I would try.

Many pressures in my office and family life prevented me from concentrated research. I collected data but didn't write.

In 1968 I attended a convention in Omaha, Nebraska, of the American History Association. I was delayed in reaching one of the big luncheons and when I stepped into the dining room 300 guests already were seated. I spotted one vacant place in a far corner and hurried there. After I had been seated the man next to me introduced himself: "I am Don Ornduff," he said. I was speechless! To have found him in that big mob was unbelievable.

By the time we had finished the luncheon I had agreed to do the article called "Culture in the Cow Country."

I sent the article to Editor Don and soon afterwards moved to California.

In 1973 or '74 Editor Don wrote me to say he had retired from the *American Hereford Journal* and had taken my "Culture in the Cow Country" with him. He was now associated with P.W. Lowell of the Lowell Publishing Company in Kansas City, publishers of exceptionally fine books. He wrote that he and President

Lowell felt my article might make a good small book. He asked though if I could suggest a different title.

"Cow Country Legacies" was the final selection. I was pleased with the book which was published in 1977 and with the generous advance royalty check.

The cover of the book--which was totally a product of Editor Ornduff and the Lowell Press, attracted much attention. The cover won an international award from the International Printers Association, Graphic Arts competition.

Donald R. Ornduff is certainly worthy of a place in Heritage Hall, not only for his editorial work but for his own creative writings as well.

GOVERNOR JOHN OSBORNE

I VISITED Ex-Governor John Osborne in his office in Rawlins, Wyoming, in the late 1930's. We had talked only a few minutes when he pulled out a drawer in his desk and took two moccasins made from the skin of the chest of "Big Nose" George Parrot, who had been hanged in Rawlins in 1884.

"Big Nose" George and his partner "Dutch" Charlie Burris had been in a train robbery in 1879 and had shot and killed a popular law officer named Widdowfield, who was in a posse trailing them. The outlaws escaped then, but later were caught. "Dutch" Charlie was taken from a train by a mob and hanged in Carbon, Wyoming. "Big Nose" was apprehended in Montana and brought to the penitentiary in Rawlins. He tried to escape from there but was foiled by Mrs. Rankin, the warden's wife. A mob hanged him promptly.

Dr. Osborne shook his head slowly. "I asked for the skin from his chest and I told 'em to leave the nipples on, but they didn't."

Dr. Osborne said he thought the United States Government paid Parrot's widow quite a sum because of his death. She was living in France.

He suggested that I talk with Dr. Heath, who lived in a large log house down Main Street. When Dr. Heath opened her door and found that I was interested in "Big Nose" George, she pointed to a piece of a skull which she was using as a door stop. "It was his," she stated.

Dr. Heath told me she had assisted in the autopsy and that the doctor had Parrot's bones preserved in a pickle barrel.

"Big Nose was captured in Montana," she said. "He was brought to the penitentiary here in Rawlins. One day he attacked a guard and got his keys. He was about to escape when the warden's wife slammed a prison door shut which prevented his escape."

I found an item in a *Carbon County Journal* which was published soon after the hanging:

"Anyone who says I put the rope around his neck is a liar." Signed ___

One newspaper carried an item which gave the size of the rope used in the hanging.

G. EDWARD PENDRAY

G EDWARD PENDRAY became nationally known for his rocket invention and his work in electronics. He attended a small college at Jireh, Wyoming, and also the University of Wyoming.

A decade after I graduated from the University of Wyoming, I was invited to join Quill Club, which I think had been based on a journalistic group to which I had belonged. When I went to the University to join Quill there was one other initiate, G. Edward Pendray.

I have always been interested in his career. Many years ago he insisted that we would live to see a man on the moon!

Before I retired as State Historian of Colorado, I was asked by a motion picture company to name several persons of national prominence to be invited to a big premiere scheduled for Denver. I nominated G. Edward Pendray and Mrs. Nellie Tayloe Ross, first woman governor, and later director of the U.S. Mint.

According to the newspapers, both attended that premiere.

GENERAL JOHN J. PERSHING

I GREATLY admired General John J. Pershing, who had married Frances Warren, daughter of our United States Senator from Wyoming. His name had been much in our local newspapers because he had been advanced in rank over many other officers.

When I went to Cheyenne to work, I found that I daily passed the home of Senator Francis Warren which was near where I roomed.

Before I went to Cheyenne, my "boss" in the library at the University of Wyoming was Dr. Grace R. Hebard. She knew that I had never been in a larger city than Laramie, and gave me a book on white slavery to read. She warned me that Cheyenne was far different from Laramie with all of the troops at Fort D.A. Russell, etc., etc.

My landlady realized that I was skeptical about the place and loaned a small handgun to me to carry when I went daily to the post office. I carried the gun in my sweater pocket.

One evening when I was passing the home of Senator Warren, I suddenly realized that Major-General and Mrs. Pershing were on the front porch. In my excitement at seeing them, I pulled the trigger on the gun and shot a hole in my pocket. I looked straight ahead and tried to keep an even pace. Nothing happened, except that I never carried a gun again.

One evening I saw the Pershings at a dinner in the Plains Hotel in Cheyenne. They were the guests at a large center table in the dining room where I was having dinner. It was a gala evening and everyone was having fun. Those at the Pershing table had a large gilt-framed hand mirror which they passed from one to another so that they could look around the room at the various diners without craning their necks.

It was a sad day for all of us when the body of Frances Warren Pershing and the bodies of their three daughters were brought to Cheyenne. They had perished in a fire at the Presidio in San Francisco. The young son, John, had escaped.

All traffic stopped and everyone stood at attention as the funeral cortege wound its way to Lakeview Cemetery.

During World War I, I daily passed Senator Warren's home and saw the service flag in the window for General Pershing.

Several years ago I wrote the General's son, John Pershing, a businessman in New York City, to ask if he could tell me, as a matter of history, how his father received the nickname "Black Jack." He wrote a gracious letter and said that the name had been given to him in the army; just why, was not of record.

When Pershing left with the troops from Fort D.A. Russell to go to the border when Villa was on a rampage, one of my close friends, Emily Jones, married one of Pershing's men, Lt. Alfred Balsam, a West Point man. The wedding cake was still warm when it was cut, but the wedding went off with all the frills. Emily's twin, Evelyn, later married Tommy, a professor at the University of California.

WALTER B. PITKIN

WHEN I ENROLLED at the Pulitzer School of Journalism, I was well aware of the book, "Life Begins at Forty," written by Walter B. Pitkin. Hence, I was delighted to find that I would have two classes under him, feature and fiction writing. About forty-five enrolled for the fiction class. Pitkin told us to study his book on the short story. Then he gave an examination on the book and selected ten of us for his class.

Nellie Gardner of Des Moines was crushed when she was not admitted to the class on fiction writing. She said she had saved her money for years to come to Columbia University chiefly for instruction in fiction writing. She remained in the school, however, and turned her attention to financial writing. Later she obtained positions as a financial writer in various places around the world.

I thoroughly enjoyed the classes under Pitkin. I'm sure his teaching enabled me to sell fiction to the western pulps.

One of my fiction stories which I handed in as classwork was about a crook. Pitkin returned it with this comment: "Worthy of the *Saturday Evening Post.*" I sold it later to *Black Mask.*

Pitkin stressed to us the importance of using words correctly. He asked us to write a sentence using the word "lady." The sentence which pleased him most was written, I think, by Henry Beetle Hough. It read: "The lady heaved a brick through the window."

When war was declared in April, 1917, Pitkin made a trip to Washington, D.C. We understood he sought the publicity position which went to George Creel.

One of our classmates in Pitkin's class was Lenoir Chambers of South Carolina. Some years later he received the Pulitzer Prize for his editorial writings.

GARRETT PRICE

HEADLINES IN the *New York Times* on April 10, 1979, read: Garrett Price, Artist 82, Dead; Did Covers for the *New Yorker*. Mr. Price's cartoons and covers appeared in the *New Yorker, Colliers, Saturday Evening Post* and other publications during the last 50 years. Coward-McCann recently published his book entitled, 'Drawing Room Only.' ''

Garrett Price attended the University of Wyoming and drew the little sketches for the *WYO*, the Junior Annual, which I edited.

As I remember him then, he was only a freshman. He was small and wore knee breeches. But we all recognized his drawing talent and sought his help with the *WYO*.

Later I saw Garrett when he was doorkeeper of the Senate during the Wyoming Legislature, when I was State Librarian.

Garrett Price left Wyoming to attend the Art Institute in Chicago and from there became a reporter-cartoonist for the Kansas City *Star*. His strip in the Chicago *Tribune* was widely read.

During his service in the Navy in World War I, Garrett did cartooning for Navy publications.

Says the *Times*, ''According to a fellow artist, Mr. Price's work reflected a gentle humor expressed in a strong but sensitive line.''

In recent years, Garrett Price and I renewed our early Wyoming friendship through Christmas cards and letters in which he reminisced about his early life in Saratoga, Wyoming, where his father was a family physician. Garrett usually drew a sketch on his cards or letters.

According to a near neighbor of his in Westport, Connecticut, Garrett was emotionally drained by the serious illness of his wife whom he attended personally during her terminal battle with cancer.

Garrett Price deposited a fine collection of his art in the archives of the Western History and Research Center in the Coe Library at the University of Wyoming in Laramie, Wyoming.

PROFESSOR MICHAEL IDVORSKY PUPIN

ONE OF MY most interesting assignments at the Pulitzer School of Journalism was an interview with Professor Michael Idvorsky Pupin, a physicist and inventor in 1917.

Professor Pupin told me he had just invented a wireless with which he could talk to a ship *three miles* from shore.

In view of the world as it is today, talking to men on the moon as a matter of course, it is difficult to comprehend the progress which has been made since Professor Pupin's invention.

I might add here that on another assignment I went to the navy yard where I was permitted to see an invention that could shoot into the air--a so-called anti-aircraft gun!

I was appointed by President Augustus Duniway, of the University of Wyoming as a delegate to the First Air Exposition which was held in New York City early in 1917. I was invited to take a ride in a small plane, but declined. I was afraid!

WILLIAM McLEOD RAINE

TO ME William McLeod Raine topped the list of western writers, in his day. I took correspondence lessons in writing from Mr. Raine when I was living in Cheyenne. He resided then, I think, in Boulder. After I moved to Denver, I met him often in writers' groups. And when my *Cheyenne and Black Hills Stage* book was published he asked to review it for the *Denver Post.*

In 1949-1950, I was employed as a publicity writer and reader's adviser at the Sacramento Public Library, in Sacramento, California. I was amazed how many of the readers asked for "Westerns." Their favorite author in many cases was William McLeod Raine.

It was my good fortune to be on the committee of three which nominated William McLeod Raine to the National Cowboy Hall of Fame in Oklahoma City, Oklahoma.

"What," you ask? "A writer in the Cowboy Hall of Fame?"

Mr. Raine knew range life, horses and cowboys as few writers have known them.

JEANNETTE RANKIN

EANNETTE RANKIN of Montana was the first woman to be elected to Congress. On my way home from Columbia University in the spring of 1917 I called at Miss Rankin's office in Washington, D.C.

Miss Rankin was cordial and seemed delighted to see someone from a sister state. She gave me a pass to the Gallery of the House of Representatives, of which she was a member, and I still have it.

ALICE HEGAN RICE

THE CRAGS HOTEL in Estes Park, Colorado, was a favorite vacation spot for our friends and my husband and me when we lived in Fort Collins. We spent many weekends there during the summer. There was a friendly atmosphere at The Crags created by its owner, Joe Mills. He was especially interested in writers as he was a writer himself.

Knowing of my interest in writing, Mr. Mills introduced my husband and me to Mr. and Mrs. Rice, two other guests. Mrs. Rice was Alice Hegan Rice, author of "Mrs. Wiggs of the Cabbage Patch," a favorite book of mine.

The Rices were a delightful couple and she talked about her writing work and urged me to keep on writing.

"It takes work," she said.

REV. JOHN ROBERTS

I HAD LONG WANTED to meet Rev. John Roberts, Episcopalian missionary, who had worked among the two tribes of Indians on the Wind River Reservation of Wyoming for more than half a century.

It had been said that he had buried an old Indian woman called Sacajawea, who had accompanied the Lewis and Clark Expedition from the Mandan Villages to the Pacific Ocean. I wanted to ask him about that as well as to meet the man who had been paid such high tribute by the University of Wyoming, the Wyoming Legislature, and the Episcopal Church in Washington, D.C. Too, I knew he had been a friend of Chief Washakie of the Shoshones.

I had known his son, Edward (Dewy), at the University of Wyoming before he went to England as a Rhodes scholar. Also classmates of mine at the university were two daughters, Marian and Gladys. I had met the oldest daughter, Nellie, and the youngest, Gwendolyn, when they visited in Laramie. Gladys used to entertain us in the dormitory with Indian dances.

Rev. John Roberts had arrived in Wyoming Territory in February, 1883, during a terrific blizzard. His heroic conduct at that time became a Wyoming legend.

In the beginning, Rev. Roberts was principal of the government school at Fort Washakie. He held that position for many years, as well as building and managing the Shoshone Mission School for girls at Wind River. For twenty years he was chaplain for the troops at Fort Washakie.

His missionary work took him out of the Reservation as far north as Dubois, west to Thermopolis, with many places in between, such as Shoshoni, Hudson, Milford, Riverton, Ethete and Lander.

At all of the places on his circuit he organized religious services and even held many meetings in private homes.

Four church record books in Wind River, kept through the years, chronicled marriages, births, baptisms, funerals and other official acts of the church performed by Rev. Roberts.

That he had been able to work with two Indian tribes--the Shoshones and Arapahoes--on unfriendly terms with each other and whose religious teachings were unlike, demonstrated his deep understanding of human beings.

On June 10, 1932, on Commencement Day, the University of Wyoming awarded an honorary degree, L.L.D. (Doctor of Laws) to Rev. John Roberts. The audience attending the presentation rose to its feet and cheered the recipient.

"In recognition of his long service on the Wind River Reservation, the Wyoming Legislature on February 27, 1933, adopted a glowing and lengthy Joint Resolution of Congratulation which said in part:

'WHEREAS, on February 10, 1883 after braving the terrors and fury of an unprecedented blizzard, officiating at the funeral of a stage driver who perished in the storm, and saving the life of a fellow traveler, arrived at Fort Washakie, Wyoming, a young man whose name will go down through history for his service to the Shoshones.

'Reverend Roberts and his family have withstood the fear and dread of massacres and uprisings.... ' "

On February 28, 1934, a beautiful silk Wyoming flag was placed in the newly built cathedral of the Episcopal Church in Washington, D.C., to memorialize the work of Reverend and Mrs. John Roberts. In the entrance of the cathedral a stone was placed quarried from Lander granite.

One spring moring, Mr. Spring and I left Cheyenne, headed for the Wind River Reservation. A late spring snow storm forced us to seek shelter in a small motel, on the edge of Lander, owned by a rugged frontiersman, Jack Perrin.

When Perrin discovered that we were on our way to see Rev. John Roberts he said, "Rev. John Roberts is the greatest man in the world. You couldn't make people in the Lander Valley believe he couldn't go up to the God Almighty and get an answer in a minute. I see him pray when he opened the road to Yellowstone Park. He prayed for the safety of the road. There was some terrific lightning and a crash of thunder, but not a drop of rain fell. Rev. Roberts said, 'Some of you will repeat the Lord's Prayer after me.' I was tending a Dutch oven at camp that day. J.D. Woodruff, the first settler in the Big Horn Basin, was with me. I asked him when was the last time he had said the Lord's Prayer. He said it was when the Indians killed his pardner. He vowed that he would kill an Indian for every hair they took from his friend."

The next morning, Jack Perrin gave us careful directions on how to reach the Roberts' home. "You can't miss it," he said as he waved good-bye.

We had no difficulty in finding the big Mission School. I had written ahead and Rev. Roberts was expecting us. Mr. Spring waited at our car.

Marian welcomed me and took me to her father's study. She explained that he was having difficulty with his vision. Rev. Roberts was all I had heard he would be. Although an octogenarian, his mind was alert and clear.

I told him we had been delayed by a snow storm but not one as severe as he had experienced upon his arrival in Wyoming.

"Yes. That was said to be the worst blizzard in the history of the Territory," he smiled. "It took me eight days to make the trip by stage from Green River on the Union Pacific to the Reservation. I spent my first Sunday in the Territory at Little Sandy stage stop, where I chopped wood all day to keep some of the victims warm."

Then he hesitated, as if looking back a long way. "The keeper at the stop went out to look for an old trapper they feared had perished. He found the wise old mountain man safe in his tent where he had holed up in his robes and blankets for sixteen hours until the storm died down."

"When did Mrs. Roberts join you?" I wanted to know.

"In December, 1884, I went down to Rawlins and met Miss Laura Alice Brown, an English girl, whom I had met in the West Indies. We were married in Rawlins on Christmas Day, and we came straight up by stage to the Reservation. Here she has worked by my side for more than half a century."

"You must have known Chief Washakie very well."

"Yes. I baptized him in 1897 and buried him in 1900. You know, of course, that he received a military burial, with rites proper to the rank of Captain. Up to that time he was said to be the only Indian chief buried with full military honors by the United States. I'm sure you know that President Grant sent him a silver-mounted saddle which he prized very highly."

Reverend Roberts smiled frequently as he talked about the Chief.

"It was Washakie who gave 160 acres in 1889 for a Shoshone Mission School. At the school the Indian girls were taught how to maintain a home. Mrs. Roberts was wonderful with them. The boys were taught practical farming."

"Could the Chief speak English?" I asked.

"He was well versed in the English language but hesitated to speak it. Old Washakie used to say 'A man who has no friends is of no account.' "

Reverend Roberts recalled that when Washakie became ill during his last days, the minister persuaded him to go to the hospital. "I took him there in my buggy."

Washakie complained that he could not sleep in the hospital because the bed was too soft. A hardwood platform was made with a blanket stretched over it. The Chief said it was "just right."

Washakie, leader of the Shoshones, died on February 20, 1900, at the estimated age of 100 (some claimed he was 102). He was buried in the military cemetery at Fort Washakie.

We talked briefly about Indian customs, past and present, and of some of the legends.

Reverend Roberts told me that on one occasion during an uprising on the Reservation, the Arapahoes entrusted their sacred pipe to him.

"It was the most cherished possession of the Arapahoes," he said. "According to their belief, it was given to the tribe by the Creator and had been handed down from generation to generation with sacred ceremony. Few white persons have ever seen the pipe. Giving the pipe to me during that trouble was a display of great confidence."

After discussing how he had learned the languages of the two tribes, I ventured to ask about Sacajawea.

Reverend Roberts spoke briefly. First, he told me that her name should be pronounced "Sac-a-jaw-ea", accent on the "jaw." He also added that Ethete should be pronounced "Ay-the-tay."

Returning to Sacajawea, he said that he first knew the old Shoshone woman when Bazil brought her to him and left her in his care when he went on a hunt. Bazil called her his mother, but later Reverend Roberts was told that Bazil had been adopted, that the old woman was his aunt. When Reverend Roberts gave her a Christian burial in 1884, he knew nothing about her background.

He mentioned that Bazil was buried on the rocks of cliffs to the west of the Mission. I told him I had been told that men had recently dynamited some of the rocks hoping to find the medal that Bazil was said to have had, which had been given to Sacajawea by the Great White Father.

Reverend Roberts made no comment. I was not surprised he did not know about the dynamiting as the report had come to me by "hush-hush" grapevine.

"Quentin Quary," Reverend Roberts volunteered, "is an aged Shoshone. He told me that he saw the old Shoshone woman at the treaty meeting at Fort Bridger in 1868. And he insisted she was the one who came to live on the Reservation."

Reverend Roberts spoke highly of the work of Dr. Grace Raymond Hebard of the University of Wyoming faculty. He especially stressed her research work among the Shoshones.

When we concluded our interview, Reverend Roberts walked to his yard gate where he met Mr. Spring, and invited us to come back again. Then he hesitated and said, "I think you might be interested in talking to Andrew Manseau who lives near Dubois. He is a real pioneer and knew the old Indian woman."

I saw Reverend Roberts about two years later in 1941 when I attended the dedication of the memorial to Sacajawea by the Wyoming Historical Landmark Commission.

It was a colorful gathering with many descendants of Bazil and Charbonneau present. Reverend Roberts spoke briefly.

He lived to the great age of ninety-six passing away at his home in Wind River on June 22, 1949.

DR. JAMES GRAFTON ROGERS

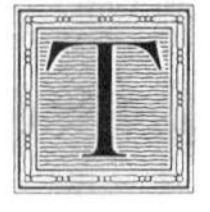

HE FIRST contact I had with Dr. James Grafton Rogers was when he, as president of the board of trustees of the State Historical Society of Colorado, called me long distance in August, 1950, from Denver, to ask me to come back from California to act as State Historian while Dr. LeRoy Hafen was away for a year on Sabbatical leave. I had been recommended by Trustee Henry Swan, who had known my work for years.

I was at the time employed in the Sacramento City Library in charge of public relations and as a reader's adviser.

Mr. Spring and I arrived back in Denver on September 1, 1950. But instead of remaining just one year with the Society, I was under the guidance of President Rogers for almost fourteen years, until I retired in November, 1963.

At his suggestion, I called him "Mister" Rogers instead of "Doctor."

James Grafton Rogers, the son of a pioneer Denver physician, Dr. Edmond J.A. Rogers, was a graduate of Yale University. In 1910 he had married Cora Peabody, daughter of Governor James H. Peabody, Colorado's governor during some of its most tumultuous years. Mr. and Mrs. Rogers had three children: Lorna (Mrs. Stephen Hart), and two sons, Ranger, a lawyer, and Hamilton, a land appraiser.

James Grafton was a lawyer by profession, an expert on irrigation law. He had been Dean of the Law School at the University of Denver and at the University of Colorado. He also had been Master at Timothy Dwight College and Professor of Law at Yale University and had held innumerable public positions. From 1931-33 he was Assistant Secretary of State in Washington, D.C. He had served on committees of the American Bar Association, and was an authority on foreign affairs.

Mr. Rogers was exceedingly modest about his accomplishments and rarely mentioned anything he had done. He did, however, now and then talk to me about being in the Strategic Command under General Dwight Eisenhower in England. I recall that he said that he did not think of Ike as an especially brilliant man, but he had a great understanding of men and could place the right man in the right place, particularly in the military.

In my first year as acting State Historian, I edited *The Colorado Magazine*, did radio and TV and newspaper publicity for the Society and did the necessary research and routine work of the office.

In the past the administrative work had been delegated to the State Historian, and then the curator of the museum during the historian's absence.

When the year was over, the board of trustees reorganized the internal structure of the Society. President Rogers agreed to assume the responsibility for the overall administrative work, without compensation. I was appointed Executive Assistant to the President, with supervision of the budget and general routine work for the museum division, the historian's office, the library and the archives.

When informing me of the appointment, Mr. Rogers said: "We think you think like a man and will be fair." Those were my guidelines.

About two days after I assumed the new duties, President Rogers left for London to preside as president of the Foreign Bondholders Security Council, comprised of representatives from fourteen or more foreign countries who were settling the World War debts.

Mrs. Rogers told me later what a thrill it was to see Dr. Rogers ("Jim") sitting at the head of the table presiding over the meeting.

He gave me a copy of the book he had written entitled "World Policing and the Constitution."

In his younger years Mr. Rogers was a leader in the Colorado Mountain Club. He had climbed fifty-three Colorado peaks that towered more than 14,000 feet. He was an ardent outdoors man. He knew the native birds and flowers and wildlife well. His book entitled, "My Rocky Mountain Valley," portrays his love of nature.

During the years I worked under Dr. Rogers' guidance, Mr. and Mrs. Rogers lived in a rambling, very comfortable house in Georgetown which had been built by a pioneer mining man. One of its excellent features was the vault built back into the mountain which housed valuable books and papers. The Rogers' home was about 45 miles up Clear Creek from Denver. Twice Mr. Rogers served Georgetown as mayor, and was closely allied to the Colonial Dames' House Museum, the Hotel de Paris in Georgetown.

President Rogers was a man of vision and he laid many foundations for progress in the Society. He initiated the Volunteers who established monthly programs for the Society and assisted in many ways.

When J.G.R. began as head of the Society there were only two field museums — Fort Garland and Healy House and Dexter Cabin in Leadville. Under his planning a stockade was built at the site of

Pike's Stockade; Baca House, the Pioneer Museum, and the Bloom Mansion were dedicated in Trinidad; an Indian Museum was built at Montrose; the large empty hangar in Pueblo became a fine museum; Fort Vasquez came into being near Platteville. Through shrewd political maneuvering plans were laid for the day when the site of Bent's Old Fort would be turned over to the National Park Service.

One of the most pleasant phases of my years with the Society was the monthly luncheons at the University Club at which the board of trustees entertained the heads of the staff. The board then was small and we felt that they took a personal interest in our work. All were prominent men in the state, and they were able to obtain good budgets for us regardless of the political complexion of the legislature. Among those trustees whom I knew best during the years were: Dr. James Grafton Rogers, Henry Swan, John Evans, John B. Kendrick, Caldwell Martin, Dr. Levette Davidson, Justice William S. Jackson, James Peabody and Stephen Hart.

In 1954 upon the retirement of Dr. LeRoy Hafen, I was appointed State Historian to succeed him. Maurice Frink was made executive director, but Mr. Rogers, as president, still retained the overall responsibility.

Mr. Rogers was always interested in *The Colorado Magazine* and encouraged me in organizing the Junior Historian Association, with a modest news sheet called, *The Gold Nugget.* He gave advice about the motion pictures which our staff produced. He told me that as State Historian I "had the right."

J.G.R. never made a snap decision. He would think things over, consider every angle of a situation and then give his advice. I saw him angry only once and that was when a staff member broke a confidence. Mr. Rogers settled the matter quickly and definitely.

He wrote songs, poetry, plays and books, plus many, many public papers. One play, "The Goldenrod Lode," was produced by the Cactus Club in Denver in 1920. He gave me permission to use a delightful poem from the play about a pony called Luck.

I have a pony and his name is Luck!
  Whoa, pony, whoa!
His gaits are tony but
  he's wild to buck
  Whoa, pony, whoa!
There's some can ride him
  like a rockin' horse
I'm pullin' leather but
  I'm off o'course.
It don't take nothin' much
  to divorce
Me an' my Luck!

Now and then Mr. Rogers' brother, Edmond, who had been superintendent of the Rocky Mountain National Park and the Yellowstone Park would drop by my office to chat. One day when I was telling of some of Mr. Rogers' accomplishments in the Society, Edmond said, (in brotherly fashion), "I'll bet you did the work."

As I look back now and realize what positions of trust and honor Dr. Rogers held, I marvel at the ease and interest with which he directed the activities of the State Historical Society. He was the GREATEST.

Mr. Rogers passed away in April, 1971 at 88 years.

"SISSY" ROOT

SISSY ROOT, owner of the opera house in Laramie, Wyoming, when I was attending school there, was known all over the West as a great bill poster. She was small but powerful. She took her place on the scaffolding beside her man helper and did her share of bill posting with her brush and bucket of paste.

She had many fine shows in the opera house as managers considered Laramie a good break between Chicago and San Francisco.

I saw Mrs. Root often as I took part in a number of amateur plays such as "The Mummey Monarch," "Road to Yesterday," "The Chocolate Soldier (Arms and the Girl)" and "Midsummer Night's Dream."

The University of Wyoming had no theater equipment so all of our big plays were staged at Root's Opera House.

"Sissy" was a sister-in-law of Bill Root made famous by Bill Nye in the "Forty Liars' Club."

"Sissy" wore work clothes when posting bills, but around the opera house she wore fussy dresses with frills and diamonds galore. We were all afraid of "Sissy" as she ruled with an iron hand and did not hesitate to swear a blue streak on occasion.

It was always a great thrill to look through the peep hole in the big stage curtain to watch the audience.

When we were playing "The Mummey Monarch," Bill Schilling, a young engineer, was seated on the king's throne. Bud Congdon, the village prankster, approached the throne, made a correct bow and then in a clear voice asked, "Good morning, king, have you used Pears soap?" For a split second it looked as if the play would fall apart, but Bill went on with his lines. Things, however, began to slip a bit. The audience did not respond to the correct lines. Bill Schilling climbed down from the throne and strode across the stage. He said, "In a few minutes I will be as dead--as this audience out there."

The cues were lost and there was dead silence on the stage. Then came a lusty round of boos and hisses. Bill walked off stage and the curtain came down.

NELLIE TAYLOE ROSS

WILLIAM ROSS, a lawyer, was one of our regular patrons in the Supreme Court Library in Cheyenne, Wyoming. He not only consulted our law books, but browsed through our magazines such as *Better Homes and Gardens.* He was a quiet, gentle-spoken man, very pleasant. I enjoyed talking with him.

I knew Mrs. Ross only slightly.

About a year after I left the state library, William B. Ross became governor of Wyoming (1923). Following his death on October 2, 1924, his widow, Nellie Tayloe Ross became governor of Wyoming, on January 3, 1925. She was the first woman to be elected a governor in the United States. She was an intelligent woman and carried out her duties well.

"Mrs. Ross was a credit to womanhood. In 1926, however, it was quite apparent that the majority of Wyoming voters felt they had discharged their obligation to this fine woman and would elect not only a man, but a Republican," said W.C. Deming, Cheyenne newspaperman.

Later President Roosevelt appointed her director of the U.S. Mint and she moved to Washington, D.C.

Mrs. Ross was a good Democrat, but although she knew that I was a Republican, she endorsed me for a position as associate historian in the National Park Service, after I had passed a civil service examination. But even her influence could not break through the political barriers set up by Harold Ickes, Roosevelt's "axe man" where appointments were concerned.

Some years later, when I was State Historian of Colorado, I was asked to nominate two persons from the West of national prominence. I named Nellie Tayloe Ross and G. Edward Pendray, the "rocket man." They were to attend a premiere of a big motion picture in Denver. Both attended, but did not know by whom they had been nominated.

Mrs. Ross was a splendid woman and capable in office. She died in Washington, D.C. in 1978 at the age of 101.

MARI SANDOZ

HEN I WAS director of the Wyoming Writers' Project, Mari Sandoz, outstanding western writer, author of "Old Jules", came to call at my office in the Capitol.

She was very interested in the Writers' Project. She said she was working on a book called "Cheyenne Autumn." She was on her way to the Big Horn Mountains "to get the feel of the country in autumn" as that was a favorite hunting ground of the Indians.

I took Mari Sandoz to lunch and thoroughly enjoyed her stories about her girlhood. She lifted the small veil from her hat which covered her ears. The top of one ear was missing. It had been frozen when she and her brother were riding for cattle during a blizzard.

"We had to stay out in that storm," Mari said. "We did not dare go in without the cattle."

Nebraska has paid high honor to Mari Sandoz as a writer. Her book called "Crazy Horse" is perhaps one of her best, in addition to "Old Jules." We corresponded several times after her visit.

Mari died of cancer at a New York hospital in 1968 at the age of 68.

JACK SCHAEFER

HEN I CAME INTO my office in the museum one afternoon I found a gentleman waiting to see me.

"This is Mr. Schaefer," my sister Alice Wallace, my secretary, said.

"Not 'Shane' Schaefer?" I asked.

"Yes," he laughed. "That's me."

His motion picture, "Shane" was one of the best.

We had a little visit in which Jack Schaefer said he decided he would like to live in Gunnison, Colorado. But on his way there, he passed through the area near Santa Fe, New Mexico, and decided to locate there. He bought a ranch and settled down.

He had come to the Colorado Historical Society to obtain information about long distance races by horseback. We were able to help some and later sent additional data to him. As a western writer, he stood tall in the saddle.

M. LINCOLN SCHUSTER

MAX SCHUSTER and Bob Simon were seniors in the Pulitzer School of Journalism when I was a junior. The seniors ran the school newspaper called *The Blot.* Because I was only able to attend the school for a year, they permitted me to take assignments for *The Blot.*

One assignment which Max Schuster gave me was to act as sports editor for *The Blot.* He gave me two tickets to cover the crucial game of the World's Baseball Series. I did not know enough about baseball to cover the game, so I gave the tickets to one of the seniors to do the report.

But when I later received an assignment to cover the All-American-Canadian hockey game at St. Nicholas rink, I went to the library and read about hockey in the Britannica Encyclopedia.

With my S. of J. press card, I was admitted to the press box at the hockey game. The reporter sitting next to me was from the *New York Times*. I told him I didn't know anything about hockey but was supposed to report the game. He said, "Don't worry. I'll give you my notes." He did.

World War I disrupted the school and I returned to Wyoming. In the mid-twenties I made a trip to New York. I dropped by the offices of the publishers, Simon and Schuster. I think M. Lincoln Schuster was then the president.

Max (M. Lincoln) told me that he and Bob had a friend in a hospital who liked to work crossword puzzles. So Max asked his grandmother if she would cut some puzzles out of a newspaper and paste them into a little booklet to take to the friend.

Later when M. Lincoln told his grandmother how pleased the invalid was with the puzzles, she suggested that he publish a crossword puzzle book. Simon and Schuster did so and cleared $50,000 on their first big venture. Their "Trader Horn" was a big success on through the years.

The books published by Simon & Schuster testify to the high standards maintained by the two men who received their basic training in the Pulitzer School of Journalism.

WILLARD SIMMS

FTER MOVING TO Denver in 1942 to join my husband who had been called to the Remington Arms plant, I called at the *Record-Stockman* office to say I was interested in writing about livestock and ranch life. I said I had just written "70 Years Cow Country," the history of the Wyoming Stock Growers Association.

Willard Simms was the editor. Later, with Forrest Bassford, he was editor of *Western Livestock*. He gave me assignments and I enjoyed working with him.

I was exceedingly pleased when he was made director of the National Western Livestock Show and Rodeo in Denver.

I'm sure it was through his recommendation that I was asked to serve on the parade committee for the show during the Gold Rush Centennial celebration. I had not until then realized how much planning, thought and work go into putting such a parade together. I was the only woman on the committee and found all of the members eager for any suggestions I could make.

It was a real thrill the day of the parade to see the men and women riders with their beautiful horses, including the Arabians with silver trappings, fall into line as we had planned. Old timey wagons, chuck wagons, buckboards, a surrey with the fringe on top, all were there. A military and other bands did their share to make the parade a success.

Willard Evan Simms retired in 1978 after 23 years as the boss of the National Western Livestock and Rodeo Show, proclaimed to be the best in the country. Willard was an excellent businessman. The show never lost money under his direction. He was born on June 28, 1912, in Meeker, Rio Blanco County, Colorado, of pioneer parents, in a far northwest corner of the state. Both of his grandparents were also ranchers.

I knew Thirza Simms, Willard's wife, in our Denver Woman's Press Club. Her home was in London before she came to Colorado and married Simms in 1941.

Although Willard Simms headed such an action-filled establishment he was "gentle and kind but firm in his dealings."

More than 20,000 entries from 40 states and Canada were registered on the million-dollar auction, 4H and FFA events, with working and performing classes, hunters, jumpers, harness, quarter horses, Arabians, Appaloosas, pintos, and Morgans in the special arena events. Willard Simms' friends are numbered by thousands.

COLONEL GEORGE SLINEY

COLONEL GEORGE SLINEY, U.S. Army, was Adjutant General of the Wyoming National Guard when I was in the state library at Cheyenne. The Colonel was a rugged, jolly gentleman who wheezed when he laughed and that was often. He had time on his hands and made the rounds in the Capitol to visit with officials and employees.

He was a frequent visitor in the state library and I enjoyed his reminiscences of his early army days. He had been with General Merritt's expedition into Indian country.

The day before he retired, the Colonel sent word around that he intended to kiss all of the girls in the Capitol good-bye.

I went downtown and purchased a leather dog muzzle. The next day when I heard that the Colonel was making the rounds, I strapped on the dog muzzle over my face. When the Colonel came in and saw me he almost exploded with laughter. The legislature was in session upstairs and word of the little incident reached up there.

Almost fifty years later I received a letter from the Colonel's son-in-law, Fred Holdrege, who had been a member of that legislature. I had known him through the years. He wrote: "I served on the Wyoming Legislature for several years, but the only thing I remember about those days was when you greeted the Colonel wearing that dog muzzle."

DR. E.E. SLOSSON

DR. E.E. SLOSSON, one-time professor of chemistry at the University of Wyoming, had a son Preston, an unusually bright youngster, who played with our neighborhood gang but would go home early to "study his Greek lesson," being taught by his mother who was chaplain at the state penitentiary in Laramie. Dr. Slosson left Laramie to assume the duties of editor of *The Independent Magazine* in New York City.

I was surprised and pleased to find that Dr. Slosson was a lecturer on special feature writing at the Pulitzer School of Journalism, also. When one of my first assignments under him came back with a rather low grade I crushed it preparatory to putting it in the wastebasket. Dr. Slosson saw me and stopped his lecture. He said we should never destroy any of our creative work. We should save it. Someday we might find use for it.

The Slossons lived a few blocks from Columbia University and Mrs. Slosson entertained Kay Bennitt and me at tea one afternoon. Preston had grown up by that time and entertained us with pictures of himself taken in Laramie. I understood that when President Wilson went to the Peace Conference, Preston Slosson had charge of the library which the President took along.

Dr. Slosson invited Kay and me to go with him to a reception in the Metropolitan Museum of Art. It was a formal affair and we dressed in evening dresses. There were some beautifully-gowned guests present.

During the evening Dr. Slosson introduced Dr. Kunz, a good friend, who took us to a vault to see his magnificent jade collection which was on display that night.

Through strange coincidence I met at the reception Dr. and Mrs. Quimby, who had let me explore the battleships *U.S. Connecticut* and *U.S. Wyoming* when the fleet was in the Hudson for the Army-Navy football game in the fall of 1916. No doubt they were as surprised to see me as I was to see them.

MAY BONFILS BERRYMAN STANTON

AY BONFILS BERRYMAN STANTON, daughter of Frederick G. Bonfils, co-owner of the *Denver Post*, and sister of Helen Bonfils, lived on her 750-acre estate, Belmar, at W. Alameda and Wadsworth, Denver.

The white marble mansion resembled the French Trianon. May Bonfils Berryman had traveled abroad and had studied music in France. She was an accomplished pianist. Her hobby for many years was collecting precious stones and rare jewelry. She had assembled her collection of jewelry quietly, and few, even close friends, were privileged to view the collection.

I became interested in Belmar when Countess Murat's cabin was moved there. The old cabin, Denver's oldest building still standing, was scheduled to be demolished when Joseph Emerson Smith, a well-known newspaperman, persuaded his friend, May Bonfils, to save the cabin by moving it out to her estate.

When Henry Swan, a trustee of the State Historical Society of Colorado, heard me express a desire to inspect the cabin, he asked a mutual friend, Mrs. Ora Haley, if she could arrange to have us go to Belmar.

Mrs. Haley accompanied Mr. and Mrs. Swan and me, one afternoon in 1959, to see May Bonfils Stanton.

Her husband, Charles E. Stanton, met us at the house with his car for a tour of the grounds. Mrs. Haley went inside to visit with May. The estate grounds were beautiful with marble statues, trimmed hedges, flower beds and a pond. Deer, pheasants, and other wildlife were visible.

The Murat cabin, across the estate from the house, had been restored to its original state. Inside it was furnished with rustic furniture and Navajo rugs. On the wall was an oil painting of a man. Could it be Count Murat? No one could say. It was in the old cabin when it was moved. The cabin was well-equipped with electric burglar alarms to prevent vandalism.

Mr. Stanton was very gracious and knowing that we were friends of Mrs. Haley talked freely with us. He said he had worked with Mrs. Berryman redoing parts of her house and changing some of the interior decorating. He is an architect and interior decorator. He said that May was pleased with his work and had come to trust him in business matters. Their interests were similar. Both had knowledge of arts and antiques and they liked to travel.

May told him that she was not well, that she needed someone to look after her business who would have an interest in it. She suggested they be married so he could look after her the way she wished. And, although there was quite a difference in their ages, they were married.

A splendid account of the Bonfils' family life and the difficulties which May encountered as the daughter of Frederick G. Bonfils can be found in the book "Thunder In the Rockies" by Bill Hosokawa.

When Mr. Stanton took Mr. and Mrs. Swan and me into the

house, we paused to see the exquisite little shrine just off the entryway. Then we went into the big drawing room to meet May Bonfils Stanton.

She was very cordial and explained that she had wanted Mrs. Haley to see her jewelry so she was wearing many of the pieces.

Suspended as a necklace was the world-famous Idol's Eye, a 70.9 carat diamond! It was the star of her more than $3,000,000 collection. The Eye was flanked by 41 round diamonds and 45 baguette diamonds. The Idol's Eye, nearly four centuries old, had been the property of kings and princes. Its whereabouts had been unknown for ages until it was discovered as the eye of an idol.

Mrs. Stanton was wearing rings and bracelets set with diamonds, garnets, emeralds, pearls and other stones.

A servant served cocktails and delicacies while we chatted about the jewelry, paintings, orientals and antiques in the room.

Mrs. Stanton also talked about the purebred sheep they were raising on the estate, which were winning recognition in the western livestock world. Mr. Stanton had shown us the sheep on our tour of the estate.

After our visit I had two telephone conversations with Mrs. Stanton. She wanted me to find out for her the age of her old friend, Joseph Emerson Smith. She said she was sure he had not given her the right figure. She evidently had known him a long time. Mrs. Joseph Emerson Smith, also was her good friend. I had tea several times with Mrs. Smith, who lived in the home that at one time was owned by the Berrymans. Mrs. Smith had served a long time as registrar of the U.S. Land Office in Denver.

Mrs. Stanton was not well, and as I recall it, had a full-time nurse when we visited her. She died on March 13, 1962, at the age of 62 leaving her estate to her husband.

The world-renowned Parke-Bernet Galleries of New York City handled the auction of Mrs. Stanton's jewelry, valued at three million dollars. Mr. Stanton kindly gave me one of the auction catalogs which was gorgeously illustrated.

May Bonfils Stanton lived a quiet life in contrast to the bombastic public life of her father, Frederick G. Bonfils.

I met her sister, Helen, only once when we made her an honorary member of our Denver Woman's Press Club.

IRVING STONE

IRVING STONE, well-known author, came into the library of our Society one morning and did some research for a book he was writing. It seemed to me the time he spent in the library was rather brief for the subject he was researching.

Quite some time later Fred A. Rosenstock, a rare book dealer and good friend of mine, telephoned me to say that he had loaned a lot of his books to Irving Stone in California to write a new book called "Men To Match My Mountains."

Fred Rosenstock asked me if I would write an introduction to the book. I said I would like to see the manuscript before committing myself.

Shortly Fred sent me the page proofs of the book, and I began reading. I found a few errors and decided this was "history in a hurry." I declined to do the introduction because I knew corrections could not very well be made in the page proofs.

What an opportunity I missed! Irving Stone's "Men To Match My Mountains" was a big success! It became a best-seller! It must have paid the author a large royalty. One never knows about the public. The one thing that I always tried to adhere to was the advice given to me by Dr. James Grafton Rogers when I became State Historian. He said: "You must always be right."

MICHAEL STRAIGHT

MICHAEL STRAIGHT, who had written a novel based on Colonel Carrington, came from Virginia to our museum library to do research for a novel on the so-called Sand Creek Massacre. He was most personable and I enjoyed visiting with him. He did not talk about himself, but I learned that he was the father of several children.

When he finished his research, he ordered microfilms or xeroxes that amounted to $45.00. I hesitated to let the library charge so much. I pictured him as a struggling author with a family to support.

Michael Straight and I exchanged Christmas cards and had some correspondence.

When his novel was published I was disappointed to find that he had fictionized some characters. That is, he had made Anthony say things that I did not believe he would have said.

At that time I was feeling very responsible for everything that was written about the Sand Creek affair, particularly because of John Evans, grandson of Governor Evans, who was so closely allied with our Society. I could not bring myself to condemn soldiers who had followed the orders of their superiors.

Michael Straight came to my office after the novel was published and for the first time, I spoke out about fictionizing history. Afterwards I was sorry for what I had said. As a fiction writer, I'm sure Michael Straight was sincere and within his rights to write as he had. I hoped he would come back so I could apologize, but I did not see him again.

Later I mentioned to my former assistant, Dr. Gene M. Gressley, that I thought we had charged Mr. Straight too much for the microfilms.

"Don't you know who Michael Straight is?" Gene asked in surprise. "He is Jock Whitney's cousin. I had lunch with him a short time ago in the building he owns in Washington, D.C. He is wealthy."

I hope Michael Straight kept on writing. He had talent. And I hope he forgave me for my unkind remarks!

HENRY SWAN

HENRY SWAN, civil engineer, banker, railway executive, trustee of the State Historical Society of Colorado, was a great-nephew of Alexander Swan, the "Cattle King." Alexander founded the Swan Land and Cattle Company which headquartered at Chugwater, Wyoming.

Henry Swan's father, Will F. Swan, born in 1848, was one of the Swan brothers.

Will F. Swan left the company and organized the Ell Seven outfit in the Saratoga Valley of Wyoming. After the collapse of the Swan Land and Cattle Company in 1889, much criticism was directed towards Alexander. His financial dealings were questioned. I have felt that much of the criticism came from John Clay because of personal feelings against Alexander.

My friend, Henry Swan, had great pride in his family and devoted much time and energy to bringing to light the real facts concerning the family affairs. He employed me to research 20 years of the Carbon County newspapers, and 25 years of the Cheyenne, Wyoming, newspapers. He personally bound all of his data in splendid files.

Henry Swan was largely responsible for obtaining a grant of $100,000 from the Rockefeller Foundation for the Western Range Livestock study under the State Historical Society of Colorado, of which I was assistant director for a brief time.

It was Mr. Swan's recommendation that brought me to the Society in 1950.

Henry Swan and John Evans, bankers, were appointed trustees in charge of the defunct Rio Grande Western Railway. They built it up into a paying business.

Mr. Swan's second wife, whom we affectionately called "Andy" from her name Anderson, was his secretary for 32 years. She made an ideal wife for him and helped him with his historical hobby. They had a beautiful estate on a small lake southwest of Denver.

I attended the twenty-fifth wedding anniversary of Henry and Andy at the University Club in Denver. The centerpiece of the long, long table loaded with delicious foods was an exotic, over-size Swan cut in ice. Realizing the importance of the occasion and knowing that Denver's elite would be there, I, who usually wore tailored suits, bought a low-necked gold blouse and a long black silk skirt and put on glittering earrings. As I moved along the reception line, Carla Swan Coleman, Henry's daughter, said, "Well, here comes Agnes all gussied up!" Needless to say I had a fine time.

Henry's son, Dr. Henry Swan, and his daughter, Carla Swan Coleman, are carrying on the historical interests of their father. They are planning to establish a small museum in their mountain place, "North Woodside," to house their family's historical treasures.

When Louise Swan Van Tassell, daughter of Alexander, died in Denver, Henry Swan called me and asked me to go to the home of Mrs. Harry English to assist her in writing an obituary for the newspapers.

Mrs. English was elderly and a flowery writer, but we managed to do an obituary, which I took to the newspapers.

Louise Swan Van Tassell had been a society belle of Cheyenne in her younger days. Separated from her husband, she lived out her life in the Brown Palace in Denver.

Alexander Swan III, who lived in California, came to see me twice in my museum office. The second time he was returning from Scotland and England where he had been gathering data about the purebred Herefords imported by his great-grandfather. An unscrupulous author had tried to blackmail him by telling him he had information that would damage Alexander's image. Alexander III wept when he told me. We had had dealings with the same blackmailer and knew how vicious he was. I tried to console Mr. Swan and told him I hoped he would continue his research and write the book he had planned.

By request I wrote the biography of Alexander Swan for nomination to the National Cowboy Hall of Fame in Oklahoma City, Oklahoma. I admired him for the great pioneer cattleman that he was. He well deserved having his name where it is in the Hall today. To Henry and Andy Swan I owe much.

R.W. THALER

I DO NOT CALL R.W. Thaler, "The Gum Shoe Kid," a "great," but he was undoubtedly one of the most interesting "characters" I met as an historian. He was a most entertaining visitor. He dropped into my office now and then. We made several tape recordings with him. He primarily was a miner in the Leadville area and had worked with Cornish miners until he could talk exactly as they did. He told us many stories about Cousin Jacks and Cousin Jennies.

He also knew Baby Doe Tabor, who was a close friend of his mother. Because of her friendship with Thaler's mother, she permitted him to visit her in her cabin near Leadville, where she kept her lonely vigil at the Matchless Mine.

Thaler brought me two "jiggers" that had belonged to the Tabors; one was plain glass, the other was rimmed with gold. He also brought a black glass vase, which Baby Doe had given to his mother. It was a slender, beautiful vase of which I was very proud. I kept it on a window ledge in my apartment where the light could play through the glass. The window ledge was wide and I never opened the window. One day I heard a slight noise in my living room and when I looked in there lay the vase in splinters on the floor. The window was closed. No one had been in the room. It looked as if someone had taken a hammer to the vase. No explanation.

Thaler was nicknamed "Gum Shoe" when he was in Nevada. He was sleeping on the floor in a mining shack when someone stole his shoes. A fellow miner loaned him a pair of rubber boots. He rode into Goldfield on an ore wagon, wearing a cut-away coat and high silk hat and the rubber shoes. His picture made front-page news and the name "Gum Shoe" stuck to him.

Thaler laughed and bragged about being a "high grader" in Goldfield, handling ore that miners filched from mines where they worked. He told many funny tales about "characters" he knew there--Gold-Tooth Nellie, "Big Foot Susie", and so on. He "married" one inebriated couple who thought the mining stock certificate he used was a marriage license, and that he was a justice of the peace.

R.W. Thaler left Denver and went to California to be with his daughter who was a psychiatrist in a hospital, or at a university. He came in once afterwards to see us, and said he was making some tapes with some people in California. Later I tried to get in touch with him to see if we could get the tapes, but failed to find him.

He was a "character" that one could never forget.

LOWELL THOMAS

I HAVE ENJOYED Lowell Thomas' travelogues and programs on radio and TV for years.

When a new magazine called *Saga* accepted a manuscript of mine called "Arctic Gold," the editor of the magazine asked Lowell Thomas to write a bit about the story to call attention to its forthcoming appearance.

The story or series of stories had been told to me by Art Whitney, a "sourdough," who had gone to Alaska in the Gold Rush of 1898.

Lowell Thomas wrote the following column and his picture was published with it.

"ARGONAUTS ALL"

....A discussion of the new kind of gold boom and of various localities where gold is now being sought. Tells of being in Alaska several times and of his love of the North..."What really set me off on this rambling train of thought is the long story which is to be the feature of our next issue. It's a stirring narrative of one of the original Klondikers, Art Whitney, who made fortunes and lost them in the North.

"Like others of his ilk, Art doesn't believe that the surface of his Alaska has been scratched, let alone the mineral and metal resources worked out. Only a few months ago he planned to trek back there, to where he knew gold is, but serious illness overcame him. Helpless in a hospital bed that 'look of far horizons' was in his eyes as he whispered 'I'm goin' back--I'm goin' back--nothin' can stop me!'

"And that's the spirit of his story, 'Arctic Gold' which will be in *Saga* next month, and which you mustn't miss!"

The editor of *Saga* wrote:

"ARCTIC GOLD"

By Art Whitney and A.W. Spring

"Look for this big story of the Far North in the next issue of *Saga*. Art Whitney, who sat down and told his exciting story to A.W. Spring, joined the great rush of gold seekers trekking into the Klondike at the close of the Spanish-American War. Far horizons called him and with the Aurora Borealis as his rainbow he found many pots of gold — and what happened to them and him is the story. You will like this yarn of a young sourdough who suffered hardships and losses, but never lost heart, and always believed that the 'best was yet to come.' "

Saga had agreed to pay me $500.00 on publication. That was real money then.

I received the page proofs of "Arctic Gold," which had been illustrated, and I waited eagerly for a copy of *Saga's* next issue.

It did not come. No check arrived. I could not get in touch with the publisher. *Saga* had folded.

I wrote the editor and asked to have my manuscript returned. When he did not reply, I appealed to Lowell Thomas for help.

Mr. Thomas wrote me that he was in no way responsible for the magazine, that he had merely written the introduction for his friend. He did, however, make a search in New York City and sent me a copy of the page proof. The manuscript was never returned.

Perhaps with Alaska in the limelight again the manuscript may someday be published.

DAN THORNTON

DAN THORNTON'S name was familiar to me long before he was elected governor, as I had followed reports of his success with his purebred Herefords on his ranch near Gunnison, Colorado.

I was delighted when he was elected as a Republican in 1950. One of my first contacts with Governor Thornton was when I received a call from his office asking if I could write a short speech for him to deliver from the steps of the Capitol. I forget now what the occasion was.

"When does the Governor want it?" I asked.

"In about an hour and half," was the reply.

It was a real thrill about three hours later to hear Dan Thornton's voice over a loud speaker reading the words I had hurriedly written.

I enjoyed working under Governor Thornton. He had progressive ideas and realized that Colorado was on the threshold of a population boom.

I served on his Committee on Tourism. We tried not only to tell others about Colorado, but tried to get the folks at home to learn more about Colorado to tell visitors.

The Governor called a meeting of representatives from all parts of the state to discuss tourism and hospitality. The meeting convened in the House of Representatives. I do not recall who presided. All I remember now is that things were dragging. Attention was lagging. I was called on to speak. I said Colorado had always been known for its hospitality. And to illustrate my point, I quoted something which an old timer had sent in as fact to the State Historical Society. According to his story, Maggie Baggs, a ranch woman, used to ride the roundup with her cowboys and do her share of the work.

One night when the roundup was camped during a severe storm, a stranger walked in. He had no bedroll or equipment. He asked if he could stay all night. No one spoke up. Then Maggie rose to the occasion.

"You can sleep with me," she said.

After supper when the bedrolls were unstrapped and rolled out, Maggie laid a six-shooter in the middle of her roll and said to the stranger. "Now you stay over on your own side!"

That shook the meeting. I don't think it was the story so much as it was that the State Historian would tell it. There was a buzz of conversation and folks began to get acquainted. The hospitality meeting was a real success.

Dan Thornton's office was good to our Historical Society budgetwise and we tried to cooperate with the governor.

At a political campaign meeting held by the Young Republicans before Dan ran for the second term, a prize was offered for a slogan. My slogan, "Dan's My Man," won.

After I had retired and was doing research on a grant at the Huntington Library and Art Gallery in San Marino, California, I stayed at the Cal Tech Club, the Atheneum, and walked each morning to the Huntington. I passed many attractive homes with beautiful gardens. The place that attracted me most was lovely. I stopped one morning to ask the gardener who owned the place.

"Did you ever hear of Dan Thornton?" he asked.

I reached in my billfold and took out a card with Dan's photograph on it. It was my official identification card which he had issued to me as State Historian some years before.

"Dan's mother-in-law, Jessie's mother, owns this place," he said.

After I moved from Denver I did not know that Jessie Thornton had died of cancer, nor that Dan had remarried. I was shocked to learn of Dan Thornton's death on January 18, 1976, at his home in Monterey Valley in California.

RUSSELL THORP

I FIRST MET Russell Thorp when I called at the headquarters office of the Wyoming Stock Growers Association in Cheyenne, Wyoming. I was seeking data on "rubber-tired rustling." As chief brand inspector for the association, Mr. Thorp gave me just the information I wanted. The rustling article sold to a newspaper syndicate.

Russell Thorp, Jr., was born in Cheyenne, Wyoming, in 1877, the son of Russell Thorp and Josephine Brooks Thorp.

When Russell Jr. was five years old he moved with his family to the Home Station at Rawhide Buttes, on the Cheyenne and Black Hills Stage line purchased by his father in 1883. The main stage line was run by Thorp from 1883 to 1887.

Young Thorp learned every phase of the stage business from

making whips to repairing harness and shoeing a horse. When only fourteen years old he drove a four-horse hitch, in an emergency, on the Morino to Sundance branch of the stage line. He was taught the art of reining by the best stage driver in the Black Hills system.

His first lessons in how to manipulate the lines were taught by George Lathrop who drove six pegs into the ground and attached strings to them for "practice lines."

Many an hour young Russell listened to the drivers and station attendants tell of the days of road agents and outlaws. From Luke Voorhees and Scott Davis, Captain Willard and others he heard the details of the Canyon Springs robbery and of the capture of Dunc Blackburn and Wall.

It was no guesswork on the part of the young westerner that "Mother Featherlegs" had red hair, because he and a playmate once did some scouting on Demmon Hill and dug into a pile of rocks to verify the story. A wisp of red hair was sufficient proof.

After graduation from the University of Nebraska, Russell Jr. ranched for many years near Lusk, Wyoming and in Montana. For a brand he used a wavy line with two slashes. When asked what he called the brand he said, "Damned if I know." Henceforth the brand was known as the "Damnfino."

Russell's hobby was collecting and preserving memorabilia of the Black Hills Stage line, also old cattle brands, books, reminiscences, newspaper clippings, and everything he could find pertaining to the western range livestock business, particularly the Wyoming area. His search at old ranches, deserted stage stations and elsewhere for paraphernalia produced rich results.

Thorp quit ranching to become executive secretary and chief brand inspector of the Wyoming Stock Growers Association in Cheyenne. When he found I was intensely interested in the cattle business and had grown up on a Wyoming ranch, he made his records available to me. The history committee of the Association asked me to write the history of the Association, covering sixty years. My book entitled, "Seventy Years Cow Country, a Panoramic History of the Wyoming Stock Growers, Interwoven with Data Relative to the Cattle Industry," was published by the Association on the Pioneer Press in 1942. It is now a collector's item.

My father, Gordon L. Wright, had owned two stage lines, one in early Colorado, and one in Wyoming. I had always been interested in staging and freighting. I was thrilled when Russell Thorp volunteered to place all of his material at my disposal if I would write the story of the Black Hills Stage line from Cheyenne to Deadwood.

He had account books, reminiscences, newspaper clippings, letters, many photographs--all historically valuable. As my work on the book progressed, Russell Thorp obtained from artist William H. Jackson four original watercolors to use as illustrations in the book.

In order to assist me in bringing the book to completion, Russell placed a $200 Fellowship for me at the University of Wyoming.

The book entitled, "Cheyenne and Black Hills Stage and Express Routes," was published in hard cover by the Arthur H. Clark Company of Glendale, California, in The American Trail Series, in 1949.

In 1967 the University of Nebraska Press of Lincoln, Nebraska, reprinted the book in paperback, as the second book in their Bison Series.

After retiring from the Wyoming Stock Growers Association, Russell Thorp did special field work for the American Livestock Association.

The state of Wyoming and the West owe a vote of gratitude to Russell Thorp for having collected and preserved so much rare Western Americana.

His son, Dietz Thorp, passed away in 1977, after spending many years of his life bed-ridden from an accident in the big timber of California. I understood he learned the Russian language and taught it where he lived in Palo Alto, California.

Russell Thorp lived to be 92 years old and was buried on a hill overlooking the old Rawhide Buttes Home Station on the Cheyenne and Black Hills Trail.

PANCHO VILLA

RCHER T. SPRING, who later became my husband, and a friend, both graduates of the Colorado School of Mines, were working in a silver mine in Chihuahua, Mexico, when word came that Pancho Villa and his men were on a raid. The Americans were told to flee. Archer and his friend ran to the railway track and jumped on a handcar that was sitting there. They began pumping the car and headed for El Paso.

They were making good progress when suddenly they saw that the railway bridge over an arroyo had been burned, evidently by Villa. There was nothing they could do as the car sped forward. It was too late to stop.

A miracle happened. The railway rails held and the hand car raced on. The two young engineers reached El Paso in safety!

BARON VON RICHTHOFEN'S FAMILY

WHEN I WAS State Historian of Colorado, I received a call one day from Mrs. Phipps, who said that a friend of hers in England, who was a friend of the Von Richthofen family in Germany, had asked her to try to get some information for them. She said that the daughter of Baron Von Richthofen, Margaretha V. Schelicka, who lived in West Berlin, was trying to get information about a monument which she understood had been placed in Denver as a memorial to her father. She had written to the mayor of Denver, who replied that there was no such monument.

Baron Von Richthofen had come to Denver in the early 1890's and had been an important fixture in Denver's early development. He also had written a book about the western livestock business.

I told Mrs. Phipps that there was a Von Richthofen Fountain not far from the Von Richthofen castle in East Denver. Mrs. Phipps gave me the address of the daughter and I took a picture of the fountain and sent her information about the Baron's activities.

Thus began a wonderful correspondence with Margaretha V. Schelicka, the Baron's daughter. After her death, her daughter, Daisy, has carried on the contact with me through Christmas letters.

Margaretha wrote me that her father, the Baron, brought her mother to Denver from Germany in the early 1890's. Here she and her sister were born.

When they were very small the Baron fell in love with a Denver woman — a horsewoman — and he took his wife and the children back to Germany and left them with his father.

He came back to Denver and married the woman for whom he built the "castle."

In one letter Margaretha told me about her own family. One daughter and her husband and two children were captured by the Russians during the war. They were to be sent as prisoners to

Poland. They took their own lives instead.

The "Red Ace" in some way is connected with the Baron V. Richthofen's family.

I treasure the letters I have received from the daughter and the granddaughter of the Baron. I trust that the fountain still stands in Denver.

MARTHA BULL WALN

IN 1939 I went to Tensleep, Wyoming, to interview Mrs. Martha Bull Waln, whose taxes had just been cancelled by the county commissioners of Washakie County in order to give due tribute to her as the first white woman to enter and settle in the Big Horn Basin. Mrs. Waln was then seventy-eight years old. She was a small white-haired woman, very cordial and talked freely with me.

She said she had lived in the Big Horn Basin continuously for 56 years and apparently was still in good health.

In April 1882, Martha James, a girl of 21 years, left her home in northern Wales, to take employment as lady's maid to the bride of Sir William Cairns Armstrong, the daughter of General Lushington.

The Armstrongs left England to spend their honeymoon with friends in Cheyenne, Wyoming Territory and with Sir Moreton and Mrs. Frewen, on their "76" ranch in the wilds of Johnson County, in the Powder River country.

Arriving in Cheyenne in April, the Armstrong party spent the summer there and were royally entertained by wealthy friends, many of whom belonged to the famous Cheyenne Club.

In the autumn, Martha accompanied the Armstrongs by train to Rock Creek on the Union Pacific, then went north by stagecoach to a station on Powder River where a rig from the Frewen ranch met them.

The thirty-six room ranch house on Powder River was called "Frewen's Castle." It was furnished with a pianoforte, lavish furniture brought in by freighters more than 200 miles from the railroad. And there was plenty of evidence of the skill of hunting parties in the rugs made of the skins of bear, deer and elk. (Mrs. Frewen[Clara Jerome], was the sister of Jennie Jerome Churchill, the mother of Winston Churchill.)

Being very young, pretty, and unattached, Martha was much sought-after by the cowboys and single cattlemen.

She fell in love with Frank Bull, the well-liked wrangler of the "76." And when the Armstrongs concluded their visit and left, Martha married Frank Bull.

From a sheltered existence, surrounded by wealth, she was plunged into pioneer life of the most rugged character.

On their honeymoon trip which took them from Buffalo, Wyoming to a spot which Frank had selected for a homestead near the Montana border, it was necessary for the newlyweds to cross Clear Creek several times. No bridges. In fording the stream with horses and wagon, Martha's trunk tumbled overboard and was swept away never to be recovered. The trunk contained all of her most precious possessions and clothing.

Immediate danger of an Indian attack forced the couple back from the homestead site. The following months and years were fraught with physical discomfort, hard work, sickness without the aid of a doctor, and fear of Indians. But above all Martha suddenly found that she had to face the fact that Frank drank.

He was a good worker and a splendid hand with horses. He held positions as foreman of big cattle outfits for a time. Their first-born child died without medical assistance. When their third infant became ill, Martha determined to reach a doctor.

There was a terrible blizzard raging on the mountains and the trip in a wagon over the roadless mountainside was almost unbearable. The infant died in Martha's arms before they reached the doctor in Buffalo.

Another excruciating experience which Martha had was the keeping of the frozen corpse of Sir Gilbert Leigh in her living room for six weeks one winter until his body could be taken out of the mountains back to Britain. Leigh was killed in a fall from a cliff.

The Bulls accumulated some horses and bought a small place on the No Wood where they had a garden and life seemed easier. But when Frank sold the horses and squandered all the money while drinking and gambling there was nothing left to buy food for the winter.

Martha left Frank and took the children to Tensleep. There she was in charge of a little post office and sold sundries and men's shirts and other garments for ranchmen.

She did so well with the little store that she fitted up a wagon, bought a team and peddled groceries and clothing up and down the Basin. Indians, outlaws, and animals were plentiful in the area where she peddled but Martha kept her little family with her and they were untouched. They lived and slept in the wagon and camped by the way to cook meals.

Frank came and begged her to come back to him. She refused, then called him back and decided to try again. She had always been in love with Frank.

The Bulls bought a home in Worland and started over, but it did not work out. Martha returned to Tensleep and her sales wagon. After a time Frank died.

During the years a neighbor, named Waln, helped Martha by plowing her garden and in other ways. After his wife died, he married Martha Bull. Her later years in her home in Tensleep were peaceful, happy ones.

I had talked with many pioneer women who had faced many problems and hardships but Martha James Bull Waln deserved unmeasured praise. To leave a life of luxury to marry a cowboy and face up to life in the Wyoming wilderness was tremendous.

Mrs. Waln's children all did credit to their mother as good citizens. One granddaughter became librarian of the Tensleep Library in the little town at the foot of the Big Horns.

Paul Frison, of Worland, wrote a book in 1969 about Martha Waln in which he wove an interesting background of history of the Big Horn Basin.

When Mrs. Waln talked to me in 1939 she dwelt only on the personal happenings in her life. It was an inspiration to meet her.

DR. AGNES M. WERGELAND

WHEN I WAS eight years old I went to Laramie to attend school and stayed with my Grandmother Wright and Aunt Mary and Agnes Wright, teachers in the Laramie schools. They lived in a two-story house at 715 Grand Avenue. They rented the front room upstairs to a new professor at the University of Wyoming, Dr. Agnes M. Wergeland.

Dr. Wergeland was a native of Norway, a graduate of Zurich and had an advanced degree from the University of Chicago.

Her uncle, Henrik Wergeland, was Norway's National Poet. A statue of him stands at Fargo, North Dakota. He was the most beloved Norwegian poet, not only because of what he wrote, but because he loved liberty.

Dr. Wergeland had moved her piano into the upstairs room in my grandmother's house. And when she played in the evenings I sat on the stairs and listened. She had been a student of Grieg.

Later she became a close friend of Dr. Grace Raymond Hebard, the secretary and librarian at the University of Wyoming. In 1905 they purchased a lot on Tenth Street near Grand Avenue and built The Doctor's Inn, a comfortable home with a fine yard and garden. It was within walking distance of their offices in Old Main at the University of Wyoming.

Dr. Wergeland loved the West and particularly enjoyed her summers with Dr. Hebard in their cabin called "Enebo" at the foot of the Snowy Range near Centennial.

I came to know her best when I took classes in Spanish and history under her. She was a perfectionist and was never satisfied with anything but the best. She held a little Spanish dictionary over my head for months, promising to give it to me when I learned to speak Spanish correctly.

When I attended the School of Journalism in Columbia University and enrolled in a Spanish class, I was told that my diction in Spanish was excellent. It was difficult for my Spanish professor to realize that I had been taught the elements by a native of Norway who had graduated from Zurich in Switzerland.

Dr. Wergeland was a skilled pianist. Sometimes when I lingered after school hours in Old Main I would hear piano music, and if I peeked into the large auditorium would see Dr. Wergeland playing at the grand piano.

Dean Bode of the Episcopal Church in Laramie was an accomplished organist and had a great appreciation of music. Dr. Wergeland gave him the original music which had been given to her by Grieg.

Dr. Wergeland's health failed and she died in 1914 at the age of 57.

Dr. Hebard sent for me and I went to Laramie from Cheyenne. Dr. Hebard asked me to help with the funeral.

Dr. Wergeland lay peacefully in her casket and at Dr. Hebard's request, I placed her glasses in one hand.

It was then that Dr. Hebard told me of the great struggle it had been for Agnes Wergeland to obtain an education. She was poor in her youth and really knew want before she obtained the position at the University of Wyoming. She always had a fear of poverty and bought useful clothing in quantities so that she never again would want.

In her later years her hair was prematurely white and her features looked like they were carved in marble.

MEREDITH WILSON and RENI

N 1962 WHEN "The Unsinkable Molly Brown" was playing in Denver, Meredith and Reni Wilson and their scriptwriter, Richard Morris visited the State Museum.

It was fun to see how much they enjoyed our Molly Brown memorabilia. They looked at the scrapbooks and photographs, smiled at the Parisian gown and asked questions about the Brown family. They also went by the Brown home, "The House of Lions."

Harve Presley, the leading man in the show also came and I walked with him around the museum. He was handsome and quite braggy about the ranch he had just purchased from Bing Crosby at Elko, Nevada.

The Wilsons and Morris were delighted with every bit of information they found about Molly Brown. Richard Morris came to my office and presented the working script for the play. He told me that the song, "Colorado, My Home" was not being sung in the play in Denver but that it was being sung in London. He inserted a copy of it in the script which he gave the State Historical Society.

DUCHESS of WINDSOR

INNIE BRYANT WEED, ex-wife of "Spig" Weed, author of "Wings," and granddaughter of Governor John L. Routt of Colorado, a long-time friend of my husband, Archer T. Spring, was with us in Cheyenne, when the news was broadcast that on June 3, 1937, the Duke of Windsor had married "the woman I love"--Bessie Wallis Warfield Simpson.

Archer had been a classmate and fraternity brother of Routt Bryant, Minnie's brother, in the Colorado School of Mines at Golden.

At dinner that night Minnie reminisced about the days when she and "Wally" Warfield were Navy wives at San Diego. Theirs was not just a casual acquaintance. "Wally" had stayed for six weeks at one time with Minnie when their husbands were away on sea duty.

She chuckled when she told of the gala visits she and "Spig" and their friends made to Tia Juana from San Diego.

Minnie Weed declared that Wally Warfield Spencer Simpson was the finest, most brilliant woman she had ever known. She said she possessed all of the fine qualities one could wish in a friend. She staunchly defended her against criticism, especially against criticism for divorcing Ernest Simpson.

We drank a toast to Minnie's one-time friend, "Wally" Warfield.

WILLIAM WRIGHT - DAN De QUILLE

WILLIAM WRIGHT (Dan De Quille) was my father's cousin. Their home was in Iowa. Dan De Quille's best known work was "The Big Bonanza."

Isaac Wright, my paternal grandfather, left his family in Iowa in 1865 and crossed the Great Plains on the Overland Trail on his way to Virginia City, Nevada where he assisted his cousin, William Wright with the *Territorial Enterprise* newspaper he was publishing with Mark Twain. Mark was away for a time.

My Aunt Mary Wright, father's sister, knew Dan De Quille well and used to tell me about his visit back to Iowa to speed up the publication of "The Big Bonanza." He was very distressed over Twain's slowness in getting out the book.

In my research in western history I have run across a number of articles written by Dan De Quille. There is no question about his originality nor his writing ability but he never seemed to win the recognition he deserved.

The family connection between William Wright and Mark Twain was very, very distant, but far-back a connection there was.

PETE WOLLERY

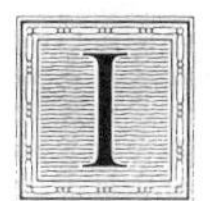
IN THE DAYS when bands and orchestras played fine music of their choice over radio, I always had radio music on when I was writing fiction for the pulps.

One song gave me real inspiration. It was written by Paul Whiteman, "My Wonderful One." This was Pete Wollery's theme song. Pete Wollery had an orchestra which broadcast from Philadelphia. He had just the right voice for that song.

I was writing love stories and I wanted to experience the thrill of having a radio singer sing a song just for me.

I wrote Pete Wollery and told him I was writing fiction and I asked if he would sing a song just for me.

He obliged. He sent me an autographed photograph of himself and said he would sing "My Shawl," for the first time on the air at a designated time.

It was a real thrill. I used the incident in a story which I sold to *Love Story*.

In a few days after Pete sang "My Shawl" for me, I received a letter from a young woman who said she was going to marry Pete Wollery in the near future.

I continued to listen to "My Wonderful One."

Years later I found that Pete Wollery was in the song publishing business in New York City! I'm sure he has been successful.